Healing the Body of Christ

Thanking God for your
fellowship over
the years

30034 45

For my four wonderful daughters Helen,
Catherine, Susan and Rachel

Healing the Body of Christ

Restoring hope and calm to a
fragmented church

Robert Amess

Authentic

LONDON ● COLORADO SPRINGS ● HYDERABAD

13 12 11 10 09 08 07   7 6 5 4 3 2 1

First published in 2007 by Authentic Media
9 Holdom Avenue, Bletchley, Milton Keynes, Bucks, MK1 1QR
1820 Jet Stream Drive, Colorado Springs, CO 80921, USA
OM Authentic Media, Medchal Road, Jeedimetla Village,
Secunderabad 500 055 A.P., India
www.authenticmedia.co.uk
Authentic Media is a division of IBS-STL U.K., limited by guarantee,
with its Registered Office at Kingstown Broadway, Carlisle, Cumbria
CA3 0HA. Registered in England & Wales No. 1216232. Registered
charity 270162
The right of Robert Amess to be identified as the author of this work
has been asserted by him in accordance with the Copyright, Designs
and Patents Act 1988.

British Library Cataloguing in Publication Data
A catalogue record for this book is available from the
British Library

ISBN-13: 978-1-85078-725-9
ISBN-10: 1-85078-725-5

Unless otherwise stated, Scripture quotations are taken from the HOLY
BIBLE, NEW INTERNATIONAL VERSION. Copyright © 1973, 1978,
1984 by the International Bible Society. Used by permission of Hodder
& Stoughton Limited. All rights reserved. 'NIV' is a registered
trademark of the International Bible Society UK trademark number
1448790

Cover design fourninezero design.
Print Management by Adare Carwin
Printed in Great Britain by J.H. Haynes and Co., Sparkford

Contents

Acknowledgements

I would like to extend my heartfelt thanks to my wife Beth, daughter Rachel and Tara Smith for their valuable assistance in the preparation of this book.

I have quoted widely throughout the book on various aspects of theological thought in the church although, as a convinced evangelical, I do not necessarily agree with everything that has been said and done. I have concentrated particularly on including commentary from writers who were at the centre of these debates (and not so much from those writing today, who comment from a distance). Two of my sources, E.J. Poole Connor and Lesslie Newbigin, lived out their Christian lives in different expressions of churchmanship, yet my appreciation for them is boundless.

Introduction

'What do you mean by that?'

We have all been asked this question at one time or another, and probably many times if we are scholars, philosophers or theologians. For theologians in particular, however, this question of meaning is vitally important.

John Gibbon, a member of one of my churches and a great friend, invited my wife and me to his inaugural lecture when he became professor of applied mathematics at Imperial College, London.

'I didn't understand everything you said,' I admitted to this eminent mathematician when we congratulated him after the lecture.

'I don't understand everything you say,' he rejoined immediately.

'But ah,' I replied, 'what I have to say is important!'

As we grapple with the concept of unity throughout this book, and with words that endeavour to express important ideas, we need to acknowledge that these are not words in a vacuum. God's words concerning the unity of the church, as we shall see, have a living, indeed eternal, importance. At this critical point in the history of the church, which is the broken body of Christ, we cannot afford to be side-tracked by a particular phrase or an individual agenda. We need instead to concentrate on the general matter of unity amongst Christians. Let us listen – to one another, yes, but first and foremost to God. What God has to say to the church is of first importance.

Fears of, and opposition to, ecumenism are grounded in a complex history which we will examine in the chapters that follow. But a positive evangelical contribution to Christian unity is essential, and that will stem from the precedents of evangelical history and from our theological distinctives. As we hold firmly to our biblical convictions and seek to live and share the gospel, our hope is as G.K.A. Bell said, 'We who believe in Christ can be united in Christ.' This book is not a plea for Christians to be part of any movement whatsoever other than to reach out arms of love and to seek understanding with other Christians.

I

Where We Are

1

The Problem

Unity. I have been thinking about unity for years as I have watched a lack of unity impair both the life of the church and its witness. The church needs healing, and I am convinced the cure is to be found in those biblical passages that teach the truth of unity. Although I am an evangelical, this book is not about evangelical unity per se. Rather, it is about the unity of the body of Christ. While readers will bring different backgrounds and experiences to this book, we can all begin from this common ground: there is division between churches and between Christians, and this should not be so.

Why should such an apparently harmless subject be contentious? Because in order to address Christian unity we need to use what are perhaps the three most inflammatory words in the evangelical vocabulary: 'The Ecumenical Movement'. But while we need to touch on this thorny issue and try to understand why it has engendered such fervent antipathy among so many, our primary task in these pages is to address the wider and multifaceted question of Christian unity. While such a discussion must address the concerns of ecumenism, this unity is not allied to any 'movement' of any sort.

As Christians we need to lay aside the labels and ask more fundamental questions: How can Christians understand each other as the people of God? How do we recognize and treat one another? What does it mean to be part of the family of God that spans the globe? Who among us can confess that we have implied (even if we have not expressed) that 'no-one comes to the Father but by us'? How do we, repenting of this heresy, instead look at each other with the eyes of Christ? While it is, of course, impossible to do that perfectly, we will discover enough clues in Scripture to give us some idea how to begin.

The summer of 2005 will go down as the year that England won the Ashes. With apologies to Australian readers for the reminder and to Americans and other non-Commonwealth readers for whom the game of cricket remains a mystery, please bear with me. I attended the Lord's Test in London versus the Australians (some of you will remember that was the one England lost!). The match was, of course, televised, and my daughter Catherine told her eldest daughter to go and see if she could see Grandpa on television. After five minutes or so she returned to ask: 'Is Grandpa in the crowd or on the field?' Nice child! And why the story?

This book about unity is not primarily for the ecclesiastical spectator or the armchair critic who cheers and groans as seems appropriate. It is for those on the field of play, for those who face the pressing question of their attitude to other Christians who have different ecclesiologies, theological interpretations, worship styles and constituencies. While, as we have said, we are focusing primarily on evangelical unity, it is a much wider question. We are not to be equivocal on truth, or careless about fundamentals, but it is important to realize that God is at work in other traditions besides my own. This is not a hypothetical debate but has critical implications for our relationships with the church across the road and the fellowship around the corner.

I try to practise this unity in my relationships with the so-called 'staid' reformed and separatist churches I still gladly minister in from time to time. Unity is a practical concern for me when I meet with, and am encouraged by, supposedly 'way out' charismatic leaders. I gain much from my relationships with the other two churches, Anglican and Methodist, in the delightful village where I am minister of a church. Ours is the one with 'evangelical' on the sign and, while highlighting the debate, it does not remove our responsibility towards the other churches in the community.

You can be sure that in a small village like ours the people are watching closely to see how Christians from different traditions behave towards each other. The people God has called us all to minister among are not interested in fine points of doctrinal difference but in whether these Christians love each other. We should not suppress these doctrinal debates and indeed, as we will see, they provide opportunities for conversation. But these disagreements should remain within the churches. Only by our love for one another and for the world will those watching us be drawn to the truth of the gospel we proclaim.

Unity is important because Christians are called to establish and maintain biblical standards and principles, but it is also a matter of particular urgency. Unity has perhaps never been more important than it is today. George Carey, the former Archbishop of Canterbury, has noted that institutional Christianity in Britain is in terminal decline. Sadly, I believe he is right. But far more important than the revival of the church in these days of religious, if not spiritual, decline, is the imperative of Scripture. Whether or not the church is shrinking, if the Bible teaches unity, and if Christ prays for it, then it is not just a matter of academic interest or denominational debate. It is a serious practical concern. Bible Christians need each other. And the wider church needs Bible Christians and Bible Christians need the wider church. This is not a political exercise, or a sterile ecumenical debate, but an outworking of theological truth.

For too long we have majored on the glorious exceptions. 'The church in Britain is OK because…' But although there are exceptions – churches that are strong and growing – the fact is that the church in Britain is not OK because the church in Britain is divided. From my personal experience, which I suspect to be as wide-ranging as any, I find it impossible to say that one group or denomination has any reason to be satisfied, complacent or unthinking concerning their place within the wider church. A cursory glance at secular society reveals that Christians, regardless of their persuasion, are making little or no impact in the corridors of power, amongst the secular media, or with the trendsetters. We need a strong, united voice to address this secular age.

We cannot speak with this voice if we continue to major on secondary issues and treat our brothers and sisters in Christ with negativism and suspicion. The world will be the first to detect the false notes in a cosmetic or 'let's pretend' unity. There are difficult theological matters to be addressed; there are times when fellowship is stretched to breaking point – yet Scripture teaches that the true church is one. Because a church claims to be one of the historical denominations does not mean that it is a true church by biblical criteria. Neither will we succeed if we try to impose uniformity. We can thank God that we are all different and express our churchmanship in many and varied ways.

But the problem comes when this diversity of expression and form, or concern with secondary agendas, detracts us from proclaiming the gospel message in a unified voice. If we spoke together, saying the same thing at the same time about the things that really matter, we would communicate clearly 'so that the world may believe' (Jn. 17:21). That sort of unity may seem like a pipe dream, but it is nevertheless an injunction of Scripture that all Christians are to take seriously.

So many churches today, even evangelical ones, direct their primary witness to social deprivation, counselling, support for the broken and mistreated, Christian education and a host of other legitimate ministries. These churches have caught the 'spirit of the age' (in pursuing legitimate but not uniquely gospel agendas) and have joined forces with a multitude of excellent secular agencies working in these areas. There is biblical mandate for such tasks, and Jesus' ministry gives us clear examples. Yet our unity, calling and mandate are not to be found here. These things are ancillary to our core calling, which is to go into the world to preach the gospel (Mk. 16:15) – and the church has lost its voice, has become hesitant to articulate its core message. Our unity is in this: our understanding of what the gospel is; the transformation that it brings about; and the command of Christ to the whole church to preach it to everyone, everywhere. And Christ also makes it clear that we will be most effective in fulfilling this missionary mandate when we work together.

The Australian David Cook, speaking at the Keswick Convention in 2005, related how genuinely pleased he was to walk over the London Millennium Bridge towards St Paul's Cathedral and see a huge banner around the dome that said 'Make Poverty History'. But he was also sad, he said, because he knew in his heart of hearts that there would never be a banner there that said, 'Christ Jesus came into the world to save sinners.' His comment was not a criticism of either St Paul's or the Church of England, but rather an expression of regret regarding our common lack of conviction regarding the proclamation of our core message. Perhaps, too, it is a reflection of our lack of commitment to the kind of cooperation and humility required to work together.

While 'evangelism' is an embracing word, it does not always encompass what an evangelical would understand to be the essence of the gospel. The age-old question 'what do you think of Christ?' is the nub of the matter – it supersedes many other considerations that are important but secondary to the centrality of Christ. It overrides denomination, sacrament and churchmanship. Our unity is in Christ, but many are apparently not prepared for that and want to tag on other things as well.

Because unity is an important biblical concept, Chapters 4 through 7, below, explore what the Bible teaches about unity. There is also an important historical element to this discussion of church unity, which we will discover by looking at the history of evangelicalism in the middle section of the book. Because unity and its pragmatic expression is crucial for the health and effectiveness of the church, it is imperative that we navigate this complex and controversial material to find a way forward.

I want to share a story I was told, in that delightful self-deprecating way that our friends in Northern Ireland have, on a visit there (the geography, however, is incidental and of no importance). A man was walking over a bridge and discovered somebody hanging by his fingertips on the wrong side of the parapet. How he came to be there was never explained, but clearly he was in mortal danger.

'Are you a Christian?' asked his possible saviour.

'Yes,' was the reply.

'Are you a Protestant or a Catholic?' was the next question.

'Protestant.'

'Are you a Baptist, Methodist, Presbyterian or what?'

'Baptist,' came the strangled answer.

'Are you a Calvinist or an Arminian?'

'Calvinist.'

'Charismatic or not?'

'Not,' said the man, nevertheless hoping for miraculous divine intervention to deliver him from his predicament.

'Pre-, post-, or a-millennial?' was the final question.

'Pre,' said the man, with the desperate realization that this issue was of no great importance in the circumstances.

'Then die!' said the man as he walked away.

A similar story could be told with many different versions, but the point is well made that we all disagree over something in regard to the faith. By and large we have grown to live with our differences (baptism, etc.). Some of our differences are secondary and others are of little importance. Some of our accepted theological norms are rooted in little more than circumstances – the homes into which we were born, the partner we married, or the particular congregation where we came to faith. Most of us inherit some of our convictions – supported by Scripture, of course. But many of our convictions are much more than some casual difference of emphasis or accident of birth. These are not to be cast aside in a quest for unity. True biblical unity does not involve a diminution of theological debate or compromise regarding the centralities of the faith.

A soldier in the American Civil War, desperate to preserve his life, wore a dark blue shirt and light blue trousers. The result? He was shot at by both sides. While I feel I may be in danger of the same fate here, I am passionate about encouraging us to think biblically in order to reach a ceasefire. We all wear different uniforms, but what we need to ask is not 'Am I right?' but rather, 'What do I do when a brother or sister in Christ, through a parallel reading of Scripture, comes to a different conclusion?' Clearly this is not limited to a private debate amongst evangelicals – it involves many others, too, and we will address this question in the pages that follow.

In addressing these issues, we will need to chart carefully through the storms of semantics and the labels by which Christians have both identified and ostracized one another. Many Christians are as convinced as I am that Jesus 'walked on the water' and that, in the words of

Archbishop William Temple, 'the tomb is empty'. I have met many people who are orthodox in their faith yet who are not evangelicals and would never want to be described as such. Why? Is their perception of evangelicals an unattractive one? Does the evangelical 'attitude' seem unpalatable? Do they not want to be associated with the evangelical constituency, which is so often fragmented by mistrust and acrimony? Does the word 'evangelical' even have a place in a world that neither knows nor cares? Has the word become a permanent barrier to unity? When the secular press confuses 'evangelical', 'evangelism', 'charismatic' and 'happy clappy', is it time to ditch the word altogether? Although many evangelical thinkers would say 'yes', I am not one of them – at the moment.

But 'evangelical' has failed as a word for self-recognition amongst Christians and as a point of reference for unity. Instead, the word has engendered a new debate amongst Christians: Who is an evangelical, and by what criteria? The word may now divide more than it unites. John Buckeridge, in a stimulating editorial in *Christianity* magazine, argues just that. Certainly the unity debate would be easier without the 'evangelical' epithet. Buckeridge has become tired of being linked with the 'ultimate 21st century swear word "fundamentalist"', and 'being tarred with US right-wing foreign policy'. Is he right? John Buckeridge quotes Joel Edwards as saying that 'evangelical' is too rich and precious a word to drop, and I agree.[2]

Definition, then, is important. The distinctive with regard to the word 'evangelical' that I see as crucial is the acceptance of the authority and centrality of Scripture. By this definition, then, evangelicals accept that authority and so they, above all people, must be brave enough, and obedient enough, to tackle the teaching of the Bible on the unity of the church. For this reason, we define and retain the word 'evangelical' here.

Unity is not, however, an 'evangelical' doctrine. It is a Bible doctrine. Someone said to me recently that a certain translation of the Scriptures was an 'evangelical' Bible. There is no such thing, of course. There is no Baptist Bible, Reformed Bible or Charismatic Bible. There is just the Bible, and all Christian teaching and practice submits to it and any credible position must be drawn from it – including evangelicalism.

How is the true church to be discovered and understood? The answer, as we will see in what follows, is to be found in the Bible. Evangelicals believe certain things about the Bible, but not the Bible in a vacuum. The Bible must be intelligently and responsibly interpreted and applied.

In light of the biblical mandate, it seems almost paradoxical that this matter of the unity of the church could be contentious. Yet, instead of being the custodians of unity, many evangelicals are suspicious of the subject. Why? How did this come about? And who is responsible? The answers are not as predictable as some might imagine. We will begin by looking at three words – 'ecumenical', 'evangelical' and 'church' – in that order, for reasons that will become apparent.

2

Slippery Words: 'Ecumenism' and 'Evangelical'

Ecumenical: It's not a dirty word!

As we have seen, productive dialogue is only possible when we have a common vocabulary. Hopeless confusion is inevitable when there is misunderstanding, and this is perhaps particularly true when we are talking about the things of God. So we first need to establish what we mean when we use the words 'evangelical', 'church' and 'ecumenism'.

The word 'ecumenism' is derived from the New Testament word *oikoumene*, meaning 'inhabited earth'. This word occurs fifteen times, mainly in Luke and Revelation. The post-apostolic church used the word to refer to the great 'ecumenical' councils for the formulation of doctrine. So that's all right then – no problem there. But at the forefront of ecclesiastical thought today is a rather different understanding of the word, associated with a 'movement' within the church. So how did this shift in meaning come about? How did the Ecumenical Movement use and understand the word?

Willem Adolf Visser't Hooft, the first General Secretary of the World Council of Churches (WCC), gives several meanings of the word 'ecumenical'. 'Ecumenical', he says, pertains to the worldwide missionary outreach of the church, to the 'relations between and unity of two or more churches (or of Christians of various confessions)', and it is 'that quality or attitude which expresses the consciousness of and desire for Christian unity'.[3] Because of Visser't Hooft's place in the leadership of ecumenism, these definitions must be counted as authoritative and normative.

When 'ecumenical' is linked to a 'movement', the Committee on the History of the Ecumenical Movement, again a definitive source on the topic, uses this definition:

> The Ecumenical Movement is held to cover those aspects of Church History concerned: (a) with the bringing of [individual] Christians of different churches together for co-operation; (b) with the bringing of different churches as such together for the purposes of co-operation (c) with the bringing of different churches into union.[4]

John Mott (1865–1955) is a fascinating figure who was prominent in the early days of the Ecumenical Movement. Having been converted under the ministry of D.L. Moody, he wrote a book with the rather optimistic title *The Evangelization of the World in This Generation*. Mott seems to have turned up at every significant ecumenical event from First World Missionary Council at Edinburgh in 1910 to the foundation of the WCC in 1947. Galen M. Fisher wrote a biography of John Mott and described ecumenism from this period as follows:

> the world-wide trends and endeavours in modern times among Christians of various confessions toward fraternal understanding, appreciation, co-operation, and unity in both the ecclesiastical and non-ecclesiastical aspects of their life.[5]

Such a definition begs many questions for an evangelical, but let's press on for now. John Mott and Dr Visser't Hooft are central to the unfolding ecumenical saga, and these definitions can be safely taken as their modus operandi for their ecumenical direction and initiatives.

For many evangelicals, however, the word 'ecumenical' carries another sense that is almost impossible to define. It is hidden in the evangelical subconscious and has become a source of fear. When not used as a Bible word but as referring instead to an ecclesiastical 'movement', the word ecumenical implies 'compromise', 'reductionism' and 'syncretism'. We will explore this movement and its history to determine whether or not this is fair, and whether it is true of the Ecumenical Movement today. It is essential first, however, to understand the word 'evangelical' and 'evangelicalism', the movement from which, in some measure, ecumenism sprang.

Evangelical: A misunderstood word

You just have to read the secular press to know how important it is to carefully define and understand the word 'evangelical'. Those who say 'I know what "evangelical" means' are to be congratulated – because not many do. To define the word we need to go back to its root, the Greek *euangelion*, which means 'good news'. This is the very heart of the Christian message (Mk. 1:1). Quite simply, 'evangelical' means 'belonging to the gospel', 'connected with the gospel', or 'conforming to the gospel'. The 'simple' meaning 'belonging to the gospel' would be almost universally accepted. It must be presumed that all Christians, regardless of their ecclesiastical background, would imagine themselves to be 'of the gospel'. So where, then, does the misunderstanding come from?

We need to begin with what the word 'evangelical' is not. First, it is not to be a 'fundamentalist', although many fundamentalists would count themselves evangelical. Neither is the word evangelical to be equated with the word 'charismatic'. There are charismatics who would not count themselves as evangelicals, even though they would agree with evangelicals regarding many of the foundational truths. Evangelicalism is not to be merely to be equated with 'orthodoxy', either – although many evangelicals tend to do this. Finally, evangelical is not synonymous with 'Protestant' (although it seems to be used in this way on the continent of Europe). So what *does* it mean?

At the most basic level, to be an evangelical is to be part of a movement that began within the church during the early years of the eighteenth century. A recent definitive biography by Diarmaid MacCulloch on the Reformer Thomas Cranmer (a patron saint of mine – hence my reading of the book!), described him as an evangelical. When critics charged that his usage of this term to describe Cranmer was 'eccentric', MacCulloch answered that 'Protestant' came later and that 'Lutheran' was too narrow. Evangelicalism, he said,

> is the religious outlook which makes the primary point of Christian reference the Good News of the Evangelion, or the text of scripture generally; it is a conveniently vague catchall term which can be applied across the board … In the nineteenth century the word was appropriated in the English-speaking world to describe a party within Protestantism and within the Church of England.[6]

I think MacCulloch is right – but only up to a point. Many within the main-line churches, holding to their various creeds and confessions, would not accept the epithet 'evangelical' for various reasons based on history and ethos. We have to look further. Neither is it correct to use the term 'evangelical' to refer to only one section or wing of a denomination, for Christians from many backgrounds and ecclesiologies reflect evangelical characteristics in forms of worship. I have noted with interest, for example, that *Mission Praise* is used in many churches that would not freely or easily describe themselves as 'evangelical'.

Christians today who embrace the label 'evangelical' would agree that they desire to be faithful to the spirit of the New Testament and they believe that their ideas, in the words of J.D. Allan, 'are no exotic, esoteric development of Christian theology'. Rather, they are those who believe that they 'simply represent the original, orthodox faith of the Church'.[7] But 'evangelical' is more than that.

John Stott is a leading evangelical statesman who, after the 1967 Nottingham National Evangelical Anglican Congress, published a document called 'What is an evangelical?'. Stott here describes evangelicals as Bible people 'conserving, preserving the unique revelation of God in Christ and in Scripture'. He describes himself as a 'conservative' theologically, but not temperamentally. The gospel, according to Stott, is

> the good news of Jesus Christ, God's only Son who entered the world and became human for us. He died for our sins, in our place, as our substitute on the cross, rose again, or rather was raised by the Father from death, exalted to heaven and has sent the Holy Spirit with great power to his waiting people.[8]

'This', Stott says, 'is good news for a new life, a new society and a new world'. It is hard to believe that many would argue with this.

The *New Dictionary of Theology* argues that

> Contemporary evangelical theology has long and deep roots. Some consider that it was primarily formed by reaction to theological liberalism, and while it is no doubt true that this conflict has frequently introduced a certain complexion to evangelical theology, its basic substance is drawn from the heritage of orthodox Christian theological formation. Evangelical theology in essence stands in the great Christian theological tradition.[9]

Evangelicalism certainly pre-dates the 'theological liberalism' of the late nineteenth century. As a movement it sprang from the evangelical 'Awakening' of the eighteenth century with a desire to demonstrate that its distinguishing beliefs are centred in the New Testament.

Evangelical belief has been codified into certain widely accepted doctrinal formulae such as the doctrinal statements of the Evangelical Alliance (EA) and the Universities and Colleges Christian Fellowship (UCCF), that set out the basic Christian doctrines. An example of such a belief statement comes from the *Baker Dictionary of Theology:*

> the Trinity, the deity of Christ, the personality of the Holy Spirit, the plenary inspiration of the Scriptures, miracles, the substitutionary or vicarious suffering and death of Christ, as an atonement for the sins of his people, his bodily resurrection from the grave, his ascension into heaven, his personal and glorious coming again, the resurrection and judgement of all men, heaven and hell.[10]

But even this statement does not cover the whole of evangelical belief, for there is nothing there that orthodox Roman Catholics and others would not also claim.

To be an evangelical is not only to believe certain doc-trines. Even the conservative UCCF states that 'a study of doctrine is not in itself enough' without a change of life – for that would be antinomianism.[11] The gospel calls us to a form of life which should accompany our doctrine and, indeed, should arise out of it', says one theologian.[12] An 'evangelical' is one who believes the 'good news' of God's provision for the redemption of humankind and seeks to live that new life in the world.

These statements of foundational truths and orthodoxy, all of which are contained in the great creeds of the church, do not, however, encapsulate the nuance of what it means to be an evangelical. John Stott makes an effort to describe this rather nebulous evangelical distinctiveness as follows:

> the evangelical faith is not some eccentric deviation from his-toric Christianity ... Our primary concern as evangelicals is to be biblical. If therefore it can be shown to us from Scripture that any of our beliefs is wrong, we are ready to modify it or drop it immediately. In fact, the hallmark of the authentic evangelical is a determination to submit to Scripture in mind and life, together with an a priori commitment to submit to anything which in future Scripture may be found to teach.[13]

It is the emphasis on Scripture that draws the various defi-nitions of 'evangelical' together.

This desire to be scriptural is both the strength and the weakness of the evangelical. Often, as we shall see as we examine evangelical attitudes to unity, their understanding of Scripture differs. But it is this desire to react biblically and theologically which is the salient mark of the evangel-ical. Since no movement lives in a vacuum, and since the debate for evangelicals is not merely an academic one, the place to work out the apparent complexities and contradic-tions is in the church.

The four characteristics that distinguished the evangelical movement that began in the eighteenth century from other streams of Protestant Christianity have been defined by D.W. Bebbington. These doctrines or emphases, which have become widely accepted, are like the four legs of a table. Any one or more of them might be true of other systems of Christian belief as well, yet if you take any one leg away evangelicalism falls over.

The first emphasis is 'conversionism', which Bebbington describes as the conviction that leads to the impetus that lives need to be changed. Justification by faith is the cornerstone of evangelicalism. 'Activism' is the second of Bebbington's distinguishing features. Converted people want to see others converted. The third is 'biblicism' – the Bible was the authority for the early evangelical's belief and practice, and it still is. The fourth, 'crucicentrism', concerns the centrality of the cross of Christ. Atonement is the cardinal doctrine. Evangelicals glory in the cross.[14]

These characteristics are so central to evangelical thinking and belief that evangelicals are intransigent at these points when they are attacked from without and, sadly, sometimes from within. James Barr criticizes all of these core beliefs. Having described the 'substitutionary', 'sacrificial' and 'penal' emphasis in the evangelical doctrine of the atonement, he says,

> Thus the concentration upon the cross in conservative evangelical religion is very marked. It supplies the key imagery ('the blood of Christ'), the haunting hymns ('When I survey the wondrous cross') [brackets original], and the centre from which lines radiate to every aspect of religious practice – to the call for conversion, to the dedication for service and sacrifice, to the command to evangelize the world.[15]

Barr, who is no lover of evangelicals, is correct when he notes that these features of evangelicalism, though they cross certain boundaries, do not further a superficial unity among Christians. These distinctives, for those who do not embrace them, are divisive and separate evangelicals from other streams of church life and witness. But they are the distinguishing marks for self-recognition among evangelicals, and they represent their reason for being a definable group within the wider church. Our quest to define our terms then leads, of course, to the church. And so we must ask: What is the church?

3

The Church

The importance of the visible church

The definition of the church is a complex matter. Everything hangs or falls here. If the church is one, then it is a wounded church in desperate need of healing. Before evangelicals can seek unity and wholeness within the church, it is necessary to understand the nature of the church itself.

In a nutshell, then, what we will see here is this: The church of Christ is real, tangible and visible. It meets in a building down the road and around the corner. It is the body of the incarnate Christ (1 Cor. 12:27), who was the Word made *flesh* (Jn. 1:1). It is this tangible church that Christ will both preserve and build (Mt. 16:18). The church is so much more than the nebulous 'invisible' and 'spiritual' concept that some have. As with the incarnate body of Christ, the church's existence is a reality. Its suffering is actual and its mission universal.

While countless theologians have examined the meaning of 'church' and have disagreed over, for instance, whether the different biblical uses of 'church' are primary or derivative, the New Testament does give us a clear picture. The word *ecclesia* is used in three ways in the New Testament. The church is firstly a particular local fellowship (Rom.

16:1). Second, it is the actual 'assembly' of the believers in any place, meeting together for worship (1 Cor. 11:18). Lastly, it is the universal church (Eph. 1:22). In other words, it is the one universal church of all time and all places (Mt. 16:18). In creedal language, it is 'the whole company of the redeemed' (as in Eph. 1:22; 5:23, where the church is portrayed as Christ's body). In its local manifestation it is a congregation (Mt. 18:17), a gathering of the Lord's people (Acts 20:28; 1 Cor. 1:2; Gal. 1:13; 1 Thess. 1:1; 2 Thess. 1:1), the coming together of the redeemed and the assembly of believers.

The local assembly is still the 'church' singular, as in 'the church throughout Judea' (Acts 9:31). When the word *ecclesia* refers to a district like this it suggests a link back to the church in Jerusalem (Acts 8:1), from which it has been scattered. Similarly, in Rome Gaius was the host of the 'whole church' (Rom. 16:23). This clearly is a reference to the church that met in his house, which was probably one amongst several churches.

When we understand this biblical picture of the church, certain ecumenical (in the classic meaning of the word, from *oikoumene*) responsibilities follow. As Christians, we are to work towards demonstrating and furthering the inherent unity of the church. If every local church is not only part of the church but is, in a sense, all of it (1 Cor. 12:12), as the indivisible body of Christ, this commitment takes on another level of urgency.

This matter of Christian unity in general and evangelical unity in particular is a pragmatic problem stemming from a theological truth. Unity is not a matter of courtesy towards those differing in one regard or another from ourselves, but a practical response to what 'the Spirit is saying to the churches' through the Scriptures. And 'the churches' to which the Spirit speaks, as we are reminded in Revelation 2 and 3, may be a motley collection. The seven churches of

Asia Minor described there ranged from those against whom there was no complaint to the lukewarm and even the heretical – yet each were considered to be churches. To deny any church today, therefore, is a serious matter.

As Bible people, we take to heart what we understand the Bible to teach and seek to put it into practice. As the revelation of God is incarnate in Christ, so we as his ambassadors seek to be flesh-and-blood witnesses of his message. The question constantly before us, as we consider the biblical teaching on the unity of the church, is this: 'What tangible difference does this teaching make?'

The New Testament teaching concerning the church, and the metaphors for the church that it uses, both establish and reinforce the church's basic unity. The church is one. It follows, then, that a fractured church is a denial of what Scripture teaches. The creedal confessions of the church confirm this: 'We believe in the holy catholic church, the communion of saints.' Yet this 'statement of faith' is little more than that if it is not true in practice. And even the most casual observer can see that the church is not visibly one.

While in his writings the Apostle Paul mainly refers to the church as the gathered community of believers in a particular locality (e.g. 1 Cor.1:2; Gal. 1:2), he also speaks of its universal dimension under the headship of Christ (Eph.1:22; Col.1:18). We know from the descriptions we have of the church in the New Testament (e.g., 1 Cor. 1: 10–17) that the reality did not match the ideal. And when applied to the church today these metaphors (which we will look at in more depth in Chapter 5) do little more than highlight the divisions within the church. Evidently the church is many, but not one. It is demonstrably multifaceted, but hardly a unity.

The church has tried to deal with its lack of visible unity by using certain theological arguments that are true but not true enough. When I began training for the ministry, every student had to own a copy of Strong's *Systematic Theology*. Strong, an American theologian from the turn of the twentieth century, said that there was 'a transcendent element in the church. It is the great company whom Christ has saved'.[16] Dr Martyn Lloyd-Jones, former minister of Westminster Chapel and an important figure in the evangelical unity debate, wrote in his valuable book on Christian unity drawn from Ephesians 4 that 'As Christians we are parts of His spiritual, mystical body'.[17] Although he is correct, to speak of the church as 'transcendent', 'spiritual' and 'mystical' does little to help a church that is in the world and divided.

When we look at the church as Strong describes it, there appears to be no difficulty concerning unity. When noone can be sure where it is or who its members are, the problem of a divided church evaporates. In this view, the church might appear to be divided, even splintered; yet its inherent 'spiritual' reality is unbroken. Its 'secret' presence is in every place that the church is to be found. So that's all right then.

But the concept of the 'invisible church' is not what Christ intended. Jesus describes his disciples as a 'light set on a hill' (Mt. 5:14). Rather than being called out of the world, the church is in the world for the purpose of being seen. This visible function of the church is, of course, manifold. J.-J. von Allmen said:

> The word *ecclesia* has always a positive implication: it refers to an assemblage of those who obey God rather than a negative conception of those called out of the world. For the mission of the Church is not that of withdrawing from the world but of being present within the world to convey to it the summons of God.[18]

To be present in the world the church has to be visible so that the world can see it – it's as obvious as that. And even where the church is persecuted, the 'secret church' is in fact nothing of the sort – as the stories of the church in Russia and China attest. While the idea of the invisible church has a long history stretching back to Augustine, it was nicely knocked on the head by J.N. Darby, of all people, who said in effect that an invisible church was as much value as an invisible light.

The pain of a divided church is real, visible and pressing. It is a hindrance to the furtherance of its mission, as well as being a scandal. If it were not for the calling of the church to preach the gospel, a fragmented church would be merely an academic concern, but to preach the gospel is its 'divine commission' (Mt. 28:29).

Other New Testament nuances concerning 'church'

While most evangelicals accept that the Bible teaches the inherent unity of the church, the reality does not reflect this ideology or theological norm. The thorny question this dichotomy begs is this: When we meet theological doubt and uncertainty, is that error of the church or error in the church? The simplistic answer, of course, is to unchurch those with whom we disagree – but I can't believe that is right.

As we have said, this pursuit of unity does not mean that differences are to be counted as insignificant or heresy is to be ignored – far from it. While some of Paul's diatribes against those who would compromise the truth make the hairs on my neck stand on end, the attitude of Paul and of the New Testament as a whole is always positive. The purpose of rebuke and censure is always for the healing of the church. Paul has something of the mind of Christ, who loves the church (Eph. 5:25) and is constantly seeking its well-being and wholeness. We keep this in mind, then, as we continue our study of 'church' in the New Testament.

The church is one

New Testament words for 'church' besides *ecclesia* carry similar implications of inclusion and oneness. Hence *panagure* (Heb. 12:23), from *pan*, meaning 'all', and *agora*, meaning any kind of assembly, refers to all believers who form the body of Christ. There is no trace of denominational division among believers in the New Testament. Although the church was one Christian community, that community was becoming increasingly numerous and diverse.

Another word, *pletho* (Acts 2:7), conveys the same idea. It means 'a multitude' or 'the whole number'. The church is the whole number of the redeemed (1 Pet. 1:8). Wherever the 'redeemed' are to be found, regardless of their name or title or their self-understanding, they are the church.

The new Israel

With the possible exception of Acts 7:38, all New Testament instances of *ecclesia* are without theological significance. The word *ecclesia* in Acts 7 is used almost as an aside to describe Israel in the wilderness. If it is correctly translated and understood as 'church', this word carries considerable significance. If the church is the new Israel, the Israel of God (Gal. 6:16), many theologians argue convincingly that the New Testament church is but a continuation of the Old Testament 'church'. The implication for the unity debate is that Israel was never rejected – it never ceased to be God's one chosen people. Certainly within Israel there was a 'secret' remnant, a 'spiritual' Israel, which was preserved and the 'church' maintained in the context of the visible Israel that was judged and sent into exile. But it was still 'Israel'.

So the New Testament church is the 'new Israel', to whom all the covenant promises spiritually apply in the new covenant (1 Cor. 11:25). As with historic Israel, the church has often been judged. Yet as 'new Israel', a 'remnant', it has continued as the real, undivided and visible people of God. The church is not *part* of the body of Christ, it is the body of Christ and cannot be removed.

The body, visible but not yet perfect

Having established that the Bible declares the church to be one, there are still nuances of meaning to explore in regard to *ecclesia*. The church is the redeemed, made up of those who are 'in Christ' (Pauline shorthand for all it means to be a Christian, e.g. 2 Cor. 5:17) and have thereby become part of the body of Christ. 'The redeemed' have no option but to be part of various denominations. Nor is the church the building, although the 'local churches' are a visible manifestation of the body. This biblical definition of church simply states what the church is – the body under Christ's headship. It does not speak to the way that various churches organize themselves, nor does it endorse any particular set of doctrines. As the American theologian Niebuhr says, writing of the universal church, 'order in the Church is not a static arrangement of its parts but the constant action of ordering by its Head'.[19]

While the biblical usage of *ecclesia* emphasizes the fact that the church is one, the texts do not set any criteria for membership. What, then, are the qualifications for membership in the body of Christ? The New Testament church was made up of those who had received the gospel, repented of their sins, confessed Jesus as Lord and had been baptised. There was nothing more (Acts 2:41–42; 8:26–40). David Holloway has written a chapter in a helpful book called *The Church and Its Unity*, which candidly discusses differences amongst evangelicals. In it he says,

> This is not because there is no concern for commitment to truth, but because the truth of Jesus' words in Matthew 13:24–23 becomes so apparent. The field, the world, does contain both wheat and weeds between them. There are also wise and foolish virgins (Matthew 25:1–13). The early church showed, right from the start, that the visible church of Christ would contain nominal believers (Acts 5:1–11).[20]

If Holloway is right, from the very beginning it was not a pure church and cannot be. While the New Testament seems to set minimal qualifications for membership, acknowledging this is not the same as saying that the church must not endeavour to be a pure and a disciplined body. Throughout the New Testament, the church is enjoined to resist error (Rom. 16:17–18; 2 Cor. 11:13; Gal. 1:8–9; Titus 1:9–14), and to be disciplined (2 Jn. 7–11; Jude 3–4). The apostolic teaching is that error is to be confronted and sin will be judged. Theological conformity, according to apostolic discipline, should be enforced and seen as paramount (1 Cor. 4:11). Yet this discipline is for the protection, not the division, of the church.

A local church that erects high walls of criteria to contain its membership and exclude others from it is not following New Testament precedents. To reject or exclude those who do not conform to a certain list of requirements denies the 'body' concept of the church. These sorts of restrictions seem to mark sects, which have authorities other than the apostolic authority contained in the Scriptures, such as the Book of Mormon. Every church has the right to draw up its own constitution, statement of faith and rule book to which members should subscribe. What it cannot do is prescribe who is a part of the universal church.

Christians rarely grasp the staggering and all-encompassing concept of being part of Christ's 'body'. 'Cross-centred' evangelicals have laid too little stress on the foundation of the faith, which is that the Word was made flesh (Jn. 1:1–14). The incarnate Christ was a real man who lived in the world at a point in history. The disciples, who became the apostles, met this man, Jesus, and were built into living stones. Jesus said, 'on this rock I will build my church' (Mt. 16:18). To be part of the church is to be part of the visible, spiritual and historic society that grew out of the incarnation, the cross, the bodily resurrection of Christ and Pentecost. The material and institutional are not peripheral or secondary, but a vital part of what it means to be 'in Christ' (2 Cor. 5:17). The visible church exists in time and space, showing and sharing the life of eternity. Paul wrote his letters to people in different places, meeting in community, who in some way that is difficult to define were themselves an incarnation, making flesh of the undivided body of Christ.

Further reflections

No evangelical can, in theory at least, disagree or fail to act upon the irreducible truth stated by the theologian Gustaf Aulen: 'The biblical view of the Church is most comprehensively expressed in the formula: the Body of Christ *Soma Christou* … The body of Christ is not to be understood merely as figurative, it describes the very concrete way that Christ and his Church are a unity.'[21] This body is made up of many disparate parts that cannot say that they have no need of other parts (1 Cor. 12:12).

Karl Barth describes the church as the congregation which is only a living church when filled with the life of Christ and only a real church when its life is based on the foundation that is Christ. 'Congregation', Barth emphasizes, 'is significant and useful only if "congregation" is specifically understood as a living congregation.'[22] This definition accords with the evangelical understanding of the church as being constituted by those who are alive in

Christ. But this very visibility of the church can also harm the church's witness. Martyn Lloyd-Jones writes: 'To give the impression that they are "One" simply because of a common outward organization is not only to mislead "the world" which is outside the Church but to be guilty of a lie.'[23] Karl Barth is no less forthright: 'The place of the church that is no longer a church is not replaced by a vacuum. Instead we have the phenomenon of the nominal church, or the church that is merely an ecclesiastical shell'[24] – which is a frightening thought confirmed, I am afraid, by much that we see around us.

In a WCC publication (and not a modern ultra-conservative piece of writing) Barth says, 'The State and society have no problem with the nominal church for it is no threat, or they might despise it as having no significance.' In fact he defends a Congregationalist church order, which he describes as the 'free congregation of the free Word of God'.[25] Evangelicals are free under the word of God – not to endorse what they consider to be wrong, or to take part in that which they consider a compromise of truth – but to build with others on the foundation of Christ what Scripture understands to be his church, in a way that reflects the prayer of Christ 'that the world may believe' (Jn. 17:21). The inevitable theological conclusion here is that, because of their professed distinctives, evangelicals cannot be other than part of the answer to the prayer of Christ. Through this prayer, the church was brought into being for its united, undivided function and purpose, and not for the benefit of its various parts – though they were many (1 Cor. 12:13–14). Clearly, however, the church has become divided.

Many factors have contributed to this division, from the first division of the church between east and west to the Reformation, denominationalism, and so on. Different opinions regarding the mechanics of structures and a diversity of inherited emphases have resulted in several churches in many localities. All these factors and more conspired together to land people in different places, under different titles, believing different things. Inevitably, these differences have bred suspicions and negativism. Many of these differences are not just historical or cultural, as we have seen, but are held from the deepest convictions. But always we are left with the theological certainty that the church is one.

The differences between churches have often been highlighted, rather than the fact that the church is made up of many parts, even as Israel had many tribes, and that the 'assembly' of God constitutes many differing peoples (1 Cor. 1:10–17). The 'redeemed' are not the structures in which they are housed or the denominations in which they are placed. But these visible manifestations of the church remain our point of reference, and it is with them that we speak. How else would one speak to the church?

A fractured church is the antithesis of what it was meant to be. John Shakespeare, who was general secretary of the Baptist Union a hundred years ago and one of the first modern writers on unity at the beginning of the last century, said, 'The fact that there are different Churches in different lands is no breach of unity, but that they do not *know* and *feel* themselves to be different is a breach.'[26] Jesus prayed that the church might be one – not to demonstrate a theological truth regarding the unity of the church, but so that in seeing the unity of the church – yes, we say it again – 'the world might believe' (Jn. 17:20–23). To deepen our understanding of Christ's vision for his church, we turn now to look at his high priestly prayer in more depth.

II

What the Bible Says

4

The High Priestly Prayer of Jesus

As we have seen already, John 17, or the 'high priestly prayer', is a key biblical text on unity. Here Jesus prays concerning his relationship to the Father, for his disciples, and then for believers in all ages, 'that they may be one' (Jn. 17:11, 21, 22). Clearly this unity for which he prays is based on the oneness of Christ with his Father. Jesus' fervent prayer is that we should be 'brought to complete unity' to 'let the world know that you have sent me'.

The world does not know this great truth and, I believe, at least part of the reason for this ignorance is disunity in the church. But who is responsible for following through to make this prayer reality? We are. For Jesus is praying for us – not for a superficial external unity or uniformity, but for a complete oneness based on the model of the Godhead. As there are different roles and functions within the unity of the Godhead, so it should be within the body of Christ – the church.

Even the interpretation of the passage, however, has been the source of divisions. People have understood it differently according to their ideas about the unity of the church. A brief overview of the history of how this passage has been interpreted and applied will be informative here.

John Shakespeare wrote an important book called *The Churches at the Crossroads* in 1918, a significant year for the church at the end of the First World War. Shakespeare comments on the words 'that they may be one as we are one' as follows: 'A fellowship more complete cannot be expressed or imagined. The oneness of the Father and the Son is a deep we cannot sound ... It is without limit and must be chiefly visible in the Church'. Further, he says, 'There are geographical reasons why there should be many folds, but there is only one flock. Perhaps no one would dispute that the entire conception of the church in the New Testament implies unity between all its parts'. Of that there can be no doubt, for the key is the unity of the Godhead.

Archbishop William Temple (1881–1944) wrote in regard to unity in John 17,

> the glory [the unity of the Godhead] may be reproduced in them – in us – *that they may be as we are one*. The possibility of this, which seems so unattainable, is grounded in the position and work of Christ as the perfect Mediator – *I in them and you in me* ... and this unity is, after all, the fulfilment of their own destiny: *that they may be perfected into one*.[27]

Although Temple did engage in conference and debate, this search for unity is not a mechanical exercise for him. It is instead about a spiritual reality, the destiny of the church within the Godhead. As Temple said, drawing his argument from the unity of the Godhead,

> We meet in committees and construct our schemes of union; in face of the hideous fact of Christian divisions we are driven to this; but how paltry are our efforts compared with the call of God! The way to the union of Christendom does not lie through the committee-rooms though there is a task of formulation to be done there. It lies through personal union with the Lord so deep and real as to be compared with His union with the Father.[28]

Temple insisted that the church must achieve spiritual unity before it can find unity in other areas. But the church's unity is not only spiritual.

A.T. Houghton quotes a later archbishop speaking on John 17 who points to another dimension of the church's need for unity,

> The world does not hear the call for holiness, and does not care for the truth in Christ. But the world has its own care for unity ... and is shocked when the Church fails to manifest it ... It is for unity in truth and holiness that we work and pray.[29]

The wider church has grown bored of the Ecumenical Movement; and the world is not impressed by a unity that is little more than an exercise. 'A movement which concentrates on unity as an isolated concept can mislead the world and mislead us,' says Houghton.[30]

Martyn Lloyd-Jones described the unity for which Christ prayed in terms of a family relationship: 'you have no choice about that and what it involves ... Though you may disagree with members of your family you cannot get rid of the relationship. It is a matter of blood and essence. So is the unity of the Church.'[31] While all families experience pressures that threaten fragmentation, and the church is no exception, the unity of the church is not an argument to establish but a truth to realize.

In nineteenth-century commentaries on John 17 there was little anticipation that this unity for which Christ prayed would ever actually be realized. B.F. Westcott, a former Bishop of Durham and biblical commentator, wrote the following in 1881:

> The true unity of believers, like the unity of the Persons in the Holy Trinity with which it is compared, is offered as

> something far more than a mere moral unity of purpose,
> feeling, affection; it is, in some mysterious mode which we
> cannot distinctly apprehend, a vital unity ... each con-
> stituent being is a conscious element in the being of a vast
> whole.[32]

Because for Westcott unity was 'some mysterious mode
which we cannot distinctly apprehend', he removed the
impetus for ecumenical endeavour at a stroke. In doing so,
he inadvertently implied agreement with certain sections of
the church today who are convinced that the ecumenical
search is a vain and pointless task. In this regard Westcott
was a man of his time. The implications of oneness in Christ
for a divided church were not seeping through. The following century was to change that – but not altogether for
the better.

The American commentator William Hendriksen understands the textual weakness of the Westcott-type position,
yet he hedges his view with an important caveat that is typical of his theological emphasis:

> When believers are united in the faith and present a com-
> mon front to the world, they exert power and influence.
> When they are torn asunder by strife and dissension, the
> world ... will not know what to make of them, nor how to
> interpret their so-called 'testimonies.' Believers, therefore,
> should always yearn for peace, *but never for peace at the
> expense of the truth*, for 'unity' which has been gained by
> means of such a sacrifice is not worthy of the name.[33]

David Hedegard, the Swedish theologian who has had a
strong influence on conservative evangelical ecumenical
attitudes, has a more 'separatist' understanding of John 17.
He argues that this unity for which Christ prayed is hidden
and secret. It was to 'be realised in an inward, spiritual

way', for in John 17 'the Lord prayed for the unity of His disciples'. The *'unity of the churches* is something quite different from *the unity of Christians'*. He continues, 'the unity of the believers is the unity of the invisible Church. All those who really live "the hidden life of Christ in God" are included in this unity.'

Dr Martyn Lloyd-Jones describes the passage as 'one of the most exalted statements to be found anywhere in the whole of the Scriptures'. Then, rather incongruously, he says: '... our Lord's statement is not an exhortation to us to do anything, but is a prayer to His Father asking Him to preserve this unity that is already in existence'. Such a statement does not derive from a simple reading of the text. The visible unity of the church has a soteriological aspect as well as an eschatological dimension. Jesus prays for a reason – not for the well-being of the church alone, but for the salvation of the world (Jn. 17:23). This visible unity, which the tense of the prayer indicates is real though not yet in evidence, is so that the 'world may see'. Seeking to present to the world the fact of the church's unity is important. The world should see the one and hear the other. It is a necessary dual witness for which the church must work, and without which much of its evangelism is rendered ineffective. But to do this the church needs a sound scriptural framework within which to operate.

5

Metaphors for the Church are More than Pictures

The metaphors that the New Testament uses to describe the church confirm its inherent, tangible unity. These metaphors are often heaped together for emphasis. A classic example of this is found in 1 Peter 2: 4–10. The overall picture, which we have already glimpsed, is of the spiritual Israel. Peter says of those to whom he writes, 'You are as the "assembly" at Mount Sinai, that place where the people became a nation – one nation.' Israel consisted of different tribes, yet each was an expression of the whole and contributed to it. The same is true of the church today. God judged Israel but never rejected it. Israel was scattered, but a remnant was restored from the nations (Isa. 66:18–23). Like Israel, the church is a 'chosen people' called from darkness into light to be one 'holy nation', the family and people of God.

Temple

Peter builds on this analogy with Israel, saying that not only are Christians the people of God (1 Pet. 2:10; Jn. 1:12), they are the temple of God. For the Jewish people the essence of the temple was both its reality as a specific place and its uniqueness – there was only one temple (1 Cor. 3:16–17).

The concept of the temple developed throughout the Old Testament. The story begins after the Exodus with the tabernacle, which was described as the 'tent of meeting' (Ex. 33:7). It was the place of the *shekinah*, the presence of the glory of God amongst his people. This is confirmed by the many Old Testament metaphors that are used of the temple (1 Kgs. 8:10).

John saw the tabernacle and the *shekinah* glory as a picture of the incarnation. Christ 'tabernacled' amongst his people, who 'beheld his glory' (Jn. 1:14). It seems that Jesus understood himself to be that spiritual temple (Mt. 14:58), and when the church gathers in his name Christ is there (Mt. 18:20). The Old Testament metaphors build towards the concept of the unity of the church as the temple of God. The writer to the Hebrews pushes the metaphor even further, from the temple itself to the sacrifices that were made within it. The Old Testament priesthood, making sacrifice for sin in the temple, pointed forward to Christ, the great High Priest (Heb. 4:14) who sacrificed himself for the sins of his people (Heb. 10:11–18). Now the church, having become a spiritual priesthood, makes spiritual sacrifices to God (1 Pet. 2:5). There was only one High Priest. There is only one church.

In the Epistles, the one church is the realization of the Messianic temple by the indwelling Spirit of Christ (1 Cor. 6:19). The church is the Messianic community, the kingdom of God, which leads to the 'kingdom' in the teaching of Jesus and elsewhere, of which John the Baptist was a forerunner. The kingdom was at the centre of Christ's teaching.

The 'kingdom' parables contain a strong eschatological dimension but also bear testimony to the unity of the church. They speak of a future separation between the true and the false. The kingdom has both come near (Mt. 4:17) and is still to come (Lk. 12:32; Mt. 13:47ff.). Only at the Last Day will the good be separated from the bad.

Body

As we have begun to see, all considerations of the unity of the church begin with the idea of the church as one body. One theologian has likened a person being received into the church to growing a new member upon the body whose head is Christ.

Ecclesia emphasizes the unity of the church, Christ's body, under his 'headship'. Karl Barth describes as 'a nineteenth-century error' the idea of the church as a 'religious society'. For him, *ecclesia* is 'a body distinguished by the call that founded her, by the promise given to those who are the constituents of this body, by the goal they seek after and the service they accomplish in it'.[35] Scripture confirms what he writes. The constituents of the church, though many, have one goal and form one body (1 Cor. 12:12–13).

Marriage

Paul develops the idea of the church as the body with another metaphor. Just as two become one in marriage, so Christ and the church become one. This is, obviously, a profound mystery. 'I am talking about Christ and the church', says Paul (Eph. 5:32).

The New Testament church embodied quite literally this mystery of fusion. It consisted of Jew and Gentile, slave and free, male and female – now one body, sharing the one Spirit, under the one Lord, united in one faith, recipients of one baptism, under one God and Father who is over all (Eph. 4:4–6).

Paul was no stranger to mixed metaphor and saw marriage as being a picture of the church and its unity. There is only one bride (Eph. 5:25–27). This picture comes from the teachings of Christ on the wedding banquet (Mt. 22:1–14) and the ten virgins (Matt. 25:1–13). Although these parables, with their eschatological dimension, do not specifically identify the bride as the church, the implication is there. The bride is the church, for which Christ will come when he sets up his kingdom. There is only one bride.

Paul also links the idea of the church as the bride of Christ with the picture of the church as the body of Christ (Eph. 5:25–33; see also 1 Cor. 6:15ff., where he further links the 'bride' and 'body' metaphors with the 'temple'). This 'bride' that Christ will one day present to himself will be 'without stain or wrinkle' (Eph. 5:27). Then, and only then, will it be a pure and perfect church. While searching for a perfect church is a vain pursuit, that is no excuse for not striving for both personal holiness and to be the local church that Christ would have it be.

Building

Paul also describes the church as a building, based on the 'foundational' words of Jesus. In a much-debated passage Jesus said to the apostle Peter, 'on this rock I will build my church' (Matt. 16:18). The clear meaning here is that the church will be raised on the solid foundation of Peter and the apostles.

Paul emphasizes not so much the foundation but the building itself. The church is God's building (1 Cor. 3:9–10), which links back to the picture of the church being God's temple. The church is built on the foundation of the apostles, the cornerstone is Christ and the whole becomes a holy temple (Eph. 2:19–22). The Holy Spirit dwells in the temple, as in the body (1 Cor. 6:19).

Take heed

Yet, both in contrast and balance to these metaphors, the New Testament understands and anticipates the very real possibility of sin, schism and error in the church. In the story of the net Jesus describes a separation of the good from the bad fish (Mt. 13:47–52). This 'kingdom' parable speaks of an eschatological future event when the true will be distinguished from the false.

Jesus himself provides the application (Mt. 13:36–43) for the parable of the weeds (Mt. 13:24–30). The 'sons of the evil one' will be 'weeded out' of the kingdom. The clear implication is that a pure church is unattainable in the here and now – because the church is made up of sinners (1 Jn. 1:9–10), and no church is immune from the effects and consequences of sin. The New Testament also speaks of the reality of spiritual warfare (Eph. 6:10–18) and the possibility of 'falling away' (Heb. 6:4–6). Heresy was not just a threat but a reality within the church (Rev. 2 – 3).

All of these metaphors point, in some way, to a visible church. Yet the church is also a spiritual organism. It is not just an earthly organization. Therein lies the dichotomy, and it would be foolish to imply that one reality does not, nor need not, impinge upon the other. As the incarnation of the body of Christ, the church is flesh and bone. But the church also serves a glorified Christ (Phil. 2:5–11), by the Holy Spirit, who though real is not tangible (Acts 1:8). The Holy Spirit's power is seen through the church. When the Spirit came down, each person in that diverse congregation in Jerusalem heard the good news in their own language. It was a demonstration that the gospel is for all peoples, who are made one in Christ by repentance and faith. Diversity is brought together in the body of Christ (Acts 2:1–13). Yet it is the church's responsibility, by the Spirit, to walk in truth (Jn. 4:24; 14:16–17). It is the responsibility of the church to order its belief, life and witness in a way that brings honour to the head.

Doctrine is never secondary to the well-being of the church (Rom. 16:17–18). Unity will never result from a careless or accommodating attitude towards the apostle's teaching. The church is an 'apostolic' church, under authority in practice and belief – hence Paul takes great care to stress his apostolic credentials (Gal. 1:1; Eph. 1:1) and to highlight and vociferously condemn the insidious work of false apostles (2 Cor. 11:13). Try reading through Paul's epistles sometime as if you had never read them before. The heat and passion of his attacks against false teachers and Judaizers are startling. False teaching is not to be tolerated.

The acute danger of apostasy is a constant theme throughout the Epistles. There was pressure from the very beginning to deflect the church from its christological and apostolic verities. The New Testament writers are vigilant because, clearly, heresy would (and in time did) grievously injure the church.

Paul enumerates the tendencies for factions and parties (e.g., 1 Cor. 1:12; 3:21). John describes the experiences of the New Testament church, with its schisms and heresies, in his first letter. The errors recorded in the letters to the seven churches (Rev. 2 – 3) tell the same story of this inbred tendency towards splintering the church.

This bias towards fragmentation and polarization is seen in the 'charismatic' excess of the church at Corinth (1 Cor. 12–14), in the naive eschatology of the church at Thessalonica (2 Thess. 3:6–15), in the Judaizers at Colossae (Col. 2:8–9) and elsewhere. Such issues dogged Paul's ministry wherever he went. John addresses an embryonic Gnosticism with the assurance and testimony that the Word did indeed become flesh (1 Jn. 1:1–4). Yet all of these vehement warnings are delivered to protect and preserve the unity of the church of Christ.

As we see from the story of Ananias and Sapphira in Acts 5:1–12, on occasions excommunication from the church is necessary for its protection. Paul confronted Peter face-to-face for the purpose of guarding against an apostate church, and the Council at Jerusalem was held precisely to avoid just such an eventuality (Acts 15).

If fragmentation is the norm for the church, is there any point in resisting it? The New Testament replies with a resounding 'yes'. The doctrine of the unity of the church should mean nothing in a church that is heretical or lax on doctrine, *other than as a cosmetic or academic exercise.* Discipline, as the example of the apostles confronting personal sin (Acts 5:1–11), party pressure (Gal. 2), domestic pressure (1 Cor. 7) and theological error (1 Jn. 2:18–27) shows, is crucial for maintaining the unity of the church.

The Ecumenical Movement, incidentally, was lax in this area and suffered the consequences. One of its early branches, as we will see, was the 'Life and Work' movement – the focus of which was the church in the world, rather than its belief. But the two can never be divorced. Barry Till, a historian of the Ecumenical Movement, said that 'the Life and Work movement ... had set out by eschewing theology'. 'It was going to be impossible to divorce service from doctrine', he admitted. Whether we like it or not, doctrine is not an optional extra for the church. 'Life and Work', the movement that coined the unfortunate phrase 'Doctrine Divides; Service Unites', has not always been an exception. Because doctrine is a complicating factor in building church unity the tendency has been to play down its importance. But, ironic-ally, this attitude only ever hinders, and never advances, unity.

An urgent call

The church is one and the churches need to become one. This is the paradox. Evangelicals have a significant part to play in re-establishing and demonstrating the unity of Christ's church.

In striving for unity, of course, evangelical Christians will disagree. Different theological convictions lead to widely divergent conclusions. Although there is only a shade of theological difference between myself and some of my trusted and respected acquaintances, we have conducted our ministries in differing expressions of churchmanship as we seek to put into practice what we believe the Bible to be saying. Yet all of us need to give intelligent consideration to the matters argued here, as well as being mindful of and sensitive to each others' convictions.

The difference between the early evangelicals and many today is this: they realized that, having come to certain theological conclusions, they ought to do something to act upon them. Theology should always lead to action and, in fact, being proactive in regard to deeply held convictions is one of the marks of evangelicalism. Nevertheless, and for reasons not entirely their fault, evangelicals became alienated from the Ecumenical Movement they helped to inaugurate. They then carried this ecumenical antipathy over into the breakdown of relationships amongst evangelicals themselves. Evangelicals became controversialists. Is it a vain hope that mutual regard could first be recovered between evangelicals themselves?

But, whether or not I hope in vain, the fact remains that all Christians have a responsibility to each other. When Christ commissioned the church 'to go into all the world' he was not speaking only in geographical terms. The commercial world, the world of politics and the academic world are but a few arenas where people need to hear the gospel. And let us not forget that our God-given commission extends to the world of the church as well.

Where do we start? It's always a good idea to put our own house in order before addressing the needs of another.

Do I need to change my attitude towards other Christians? Am I really listening to them? Or am I shouting too much and too loudly? Am I called to work in the tortured area of inter-church relationships? The call is to be ambassadors of the one church of Christ. We have some hard work and thinking to do.

6

Scripture Alone

When we talk with other Christians, it is of supreme importance to discover where their authority lies. Why do they believe as they do? How exclusive is their understanding of truth?

With the possible exception of the Roman Catholic Church and some of the sects, no one denomination, or even local church, would claim to be the 'only' or 'whole' church in a given locality. Yet some insist that, in order for a church to be recognized as a 'true church', certain 'marks' need to be in evidence – a 'historic episcopate', for example, without which a 'church' has no catholicity and authority. Roman Catholics, as well as the Orthodox traditions and the Anglo-Catholic branch of Anglicanism, would hold this view. The WCC document *Baptism, Eucharist and Ministry*, however, says: 'The New Testament does not describe a single pattern of ministry which might serve as a blueprint or continuing norm for all future ministry in the church.' Evangelicals who agree with this statement would, obviously, reject this idea concerning the 'marks' of a true church. Denominations are an ugly, unfortunate necessity within the life of the church and people's attitudes towards them differ. Some regard all groups that 'profess' and call themselves Christian as part of the true church. Some deny that the Roman Catholic Church is a church at all; others consider it an apostate church. The Roman Catholic Church holds the same view in reverse in regard to those outside its 'communion'.

Often these divisions in the church 'owe more to prejudice, personality conflicts, differences of opinion over the minutiae of church order and worship, and misunderstandings', said Alwyn Thompson.[36] The differences with Roman Catholicism are hardly 'minutiae', but even in the evangelical subconscious there has been something of a reassessment. Donald Macleod, a conservative evangelical theologian, has said that 'because of history, the reaction of evangelicals to Roman Catholics is often irrational and sometimes even hysterical'.[37] While Rome as an empire is not the threat it once was, there are still considerable theological concerns.

Inevitable as these 'differences of opinion' of which Thompson speaks are, because redeemed sinners constitute the church, these divided churches have recorded many achievements. When churches of all persuasions are alive, motivated and well led they have great power to attract people and to further the work of the gospel. But that pragmatic fact does not remove the offence of a divided church, nor deal with the question of the authority for their existence and distinctives.

Often those who enter into the debate on the authority of the church understand there to be three 'sides'. The first is the 'catholic' reliance on the authority of both Scripture and 'tradition'. The second is the 'liberal' position, of experience filtered through Scripture, often taken in the main-line ecumenical debate. The third position, taken by evangelicals, is that Scripture is the sole authority.

Protestants traditionally accept the relative authority of traditions only so far as that tradition is biblically based. The question of authority became a matter of central importance during the Reformation. Authority was 'out of the

pure Word of God, a true and distinct confession', according to Calvin. John Shakespeare has asked, 'Is it according
to the Scriptures of the New Testament or is it by the teaching of the Scriptures according to the will of God that there
should be a variety of churches, living side by side in separation from one another?'[38]

Although for evangelicals the Scriptures have a particular
importance because of the part that the Bible plays in their
belief, thinking and practice, evangelicals are not the only
ones to understand the ongoing importance and primary
testimony of the Bible. The question is whether Scripture is a
sole authority, or even a trusted and relevant authority.
Evangelicals understand the Bible to be the word of God. In
all theological debate with evangelicals, therefore, the question will be what they understand the Scriptures to say to the
matter in question. They follow in the footsteps of the
Reformation, when *sola scriptura* was first coined as a badge
of their position.

The Roman Catholic position on authority contrasts with
this view of *sola scriptura*. The Church, Catholic doctrine
says, 'is entrusted with the authority to explain, interpret
and complete the teaching of the Bible and considers the
witness of the Church as given in tradition as equally
authoritative with the Bible itself'.[39] If our foundational
principles are so divergent, how can there be any progress
between evangelicals and Roman Catholics? But the church
can do no less than address such intransigent problems for
the well-being and unity of Christ's church.

In a book springing from the Nottingham British Faith
and Order Conference of 1964, David Wright and Michael
Green, both evangelicals, dealt in depth with several of the
issues raised in the debate as to the authority of Scripture
and tradition. Their argument can be condensed into a
statement and a question. At the beginning Christ the
Teacher was greater than the Christian community which

he founded and had authority over it. Does this authority rest in the Scripture that speaks of him or in the church of which he is the head?

This question leads us into the heart of the debate – namely, the place and authority of the apostles, who were eyewitnesses of and martyrs to Christ's teaching, death and resurrection. The root of the faith and its subsequent authority is apostolic. 'No tradition that is not rooted there is normative', say Wright and Green. We need, then, to establish the place and authority of the apostles in their relationship to the church.

Establishing his apostleship was fundamental to Paul's authority as a guardian of the truth. The very features that constituted the apostleship of the Eleven were the features that Paul pointed to as his qualifications for apostleship (1 Cor. 9:1–2; 15:8; cf. Gal. 1:18; 2:2; 1 Cor. 11:23). So Paul says, 'for I received from the Lord ...' (1 Cor. 11:23). Authority is centred in Christ through the apostles. The apostles rejected the traditions of men (Col. 2:8).

In their writings the early Church Fathers still appealed to the apostles as the ground of their authority, not the church. Clement writes, 'Take up your epistle of the blessed Paul apostle. What did he first write to you in the "beginning of the gospel"?' Ignatius does not write as one claiming importance, in fact he does not issue orders 'like Peter and Paul: they were apostles, I am a convict'. In fact, Ignatius states, 'I was not empowered ... that I ... should give you orders as if I were an apostle'. He had 'taken refuge in the gospel as the flesh of Jesus and in the apostles as the presbytery of the Church'.[40] So it must be for church leaders of today, however exalted their name and function. Theirs is a derived authority resting outside of themselves, and that authority is Scripture.

This is the evangelical position. A tradition may be old or of great value in itself, and many evangelicals are content with a threefold ministry (bishop, priest, deacon) as described by the Church Fathers as normative for church practice and value the liturgies and traditions of the church. But for doctrine, the essence of the faith, it is Christ and the apostles' teaching as recorded in the canon of the New Testament that is normative and authoritative.

The word canon means 'measuring-rod', 'standard', or 'norm', and is an important concept in the unity debate. On the canon of Scripture and the church, Lesslie Newbigin says,

> The Church choosing the canon was not like a book-lover selecting a library on the basis of tastes; it was like a court sifting evidence in order to obtain the most reliable account of what really happened. The controlling fact was that Christ had lived, taught, done mighty works, died, risen again and appeared to his disciples. The appeal was to those who could claim either to have seen and heard and handled these things, or to have been in direct contact with those who had. The canon of scripture is the result of that appeal. The selection of the canon is the work of the Church, but it is the expression of the fact that it is the actual event of God's work in Christ which is the supreme and decisive standard of the Church.[41]

The appeal is not to the church that formed the canon but to the Christ who was the foundation of the church.

At the beginning the church was guardian of an oral tradition. Through the guidance and guardianship of the Holy Spirit, the church was worthy of the responsibility to write down everything that was of permanent importance. Up to the Reformation, the church increasingly accepted another authority – the traditions of the church. In an age when few could read and the oral teaching of the church could not be verified, it could hardly be otherwise. But there was a change coming. The intellectual impact of the Renaissance, the invention of printing (which made the Scriptures widely available) and the translation of the Scriptures into the vernacular created an explosion waiting to happen. And Martin Luther was but the touchpaper. Authority was the basic issue, not justification by faith. Luther found that true authority lay in Scripture, as against the authority of the church and its teachings.

The Reformation was not the time for moderation in debate, and the issues were stated boldly. Article VI of the *Thirty-Nine Articles* encapsulated the Protestant view on where authority lay. 'Holy Scripture containeth all things necessary to salvation.' The Roman Catholic Church formulated their response at the Council of Trent in 1545. They carefully defined the relationship between Scripture and tradition, as described by the historian Barry Till:

> It had been intended that the Council should say that Catholic truth was to be found 'partly in scripture' and 'partly in tradition,' which would have set up tradition as an independent authority which could add to scripture. But again the text was modified and the more neutral word 'and' (*et*) was used; this did not necessarily imply that tradition was independent of scripture; it could mean that tradition interpreted scripture.[42]

A Roman Catholic historian states, 'With this "*et*" the Council avoided a decision ... One cannot emphasise enough that nothing, absolutely nothing was decided at the Council concerning the relation of scripture and tradition.'[43] Yet if real progress is ever to be made between Roman Catholics and evangelicals, this matter is going to have to be decided, and it is ironic that a matter of such magnitude should rest on an '*et*', says Till.

It would be a grave mistake to imply that this is a problem unique to the debate between Roman Catholics and evangelicals, for there is the third position on authority. Ambiguity about tradition and Scripture is becoming a feature of the unity debate in some circles which further complicates matters. Let me try to explain.

What the Bible says about schism

Since one of the distinguishing marks of evangelicals is their attitude to Scripture, the Bible's teaching must be the basis of our argument. So we need to ask whether the Bible advocates separation from theologically 'mixed' denominations and churches. Or does it urge us to work for the unity of the church?

Jesus' prayer in John 17, as we saw in Chapter 4, is central to this question. Unfortunately, because of its very centrality to the ecumenical debate, this passage is often ignored or even 'explained away'. 'If "ecumaniacs" use these verses for their argument, then we won't!' seems to be the attitude of some. The Bible, however, makes very clear that 'schism' is a fearful thing (Gal. 5:20; Tit. 3:10). Separation, other than on the basis of false teaching regarding the gospel, is against the will of God and to be strictly avoided.

What we see in the church today, however, is very different. E.J. Poole-Conner has written a book called *Evangelical Unity*, published by the Fellowship of Independent Evangelical Churches (FIEC). In this, one of the most influential and irenic books I have ever read, he says,

> Aloofness, exclusiveness, schism – these things are as alien to our Lord's ideal of His Church as darkness is from light. It was, moreover, to be a unity which should compel the world to believe, in other words a unity so palpable as to be visible even to the purblind.[44]

In stark contrast to this present reality, Paul echoes and confirms Jesus' message on unity in the Epistles. Ephesians 4:3 says, 'Make every effort to keep the unity of the Spirit through the bond of peace.' So many Christians do not make this effort. They are careless, or at best negligent, of unity in Christ – and sometimes they are downright hostile towards it. We may make the effort to be amiable towards those who share our distinctives, but often we don't deem those who fall outside of what we perceive to be 'our select circle' worth the effort. But the facts remain: the body of Christ is wider than any of us; God alone knows who are his; and keeping the bond of peace is a Bible injunction. And my plea is that the effort should be made.

Paul does not speak here of the body of Christ as a hope for the future but as a fact of the present. Those who are in Christ are part of his body (1 Cor. 12:12–13; Rom. 12:5), a metaphor that speaks of our mutual interdependence rather than our isolation – in contrast to the impression we so often give. In Ephesians 4:13 Paul gives us a glimpse of the glorious future of a unity that is centred in mature faith and knowledge of Christ. We are to work for and towards unity with those who also seek 'the fullness of Christ'.

E.J. Poole-Connor quotes D.M. Paton:

> No divergence of doctrine or ritual or practice can destroy a union which is based on life; nor is it possible to be unchurched by intellectual error when our organic union is fathoms deeper than intellectual. Unity in doctrine is impossible, unity in taste and sentiment is impossible; unity in attainment and experience is impossible; but unity in life is not only possible: it is a fact.

This is not, of course, an argument for believing what you want, for neglecting Scripture or for reducing the faith to the lowest common denominator. Rather, Poole-Connor's point is that the body of Christ is a living entity, and this unity is indestructible.

Paul describes true unity in Ephesians 4, verses 4–5, and further elaborates in verses 14–16. These verses are also central to the unity debate. The church is not a literal physical building but the body of Christ, constructed of all who are 'in Christ'. The same God, by the Holy Spirit, works in all of us (1 Cor. 12:6), regardless of our differences. If anyone does not have the Spirit, then that one is not in Christ (Rom. 8:9). It is not for us to decide who has the Spirit, but together we 'hope' for his sanctifying work that will bring us to complete fulfilment in Christ. Sanctification is an ongoing work for all of us on this journey, and we are to treat our fellow travellers with deep respect. Everyone who calls on the Lord will be saved (Rom. 10:11–12), and it is not for us to argue with the love and sovereignty of God as to who they might be.

Paul speaks of 'one faith' in Ephesians 4:5. In this context, 'one faith' probably refers to that irreducible minimum for salvation for which Jude tells us to contend (Jude 3). For me that is the deity of Christ, his work for our salvation on the cross and his physical resurrection from the dead. All of this is, Paul says, is portrayed and confirmed by one baptism.

But there are many disagreements on this point. Once again I turn to Poole-Conner:

> Will any man outside Rome have the hardihood to claim that the religious assembly to which he belongs is alone infallible? The very fact that there are divergences should inculcate humility. The utmost that anyone can say is that his creed is a statement of Scriptural truth as he sees it and, therefore binding on his own conscience. To attempt to make it binding on that of his brethren, and to exclude them from communion because their interpretation of the 'one

faith' is different from his, is to claim for an exegesis of Scripture the infallibility of Scripture itself.

How, then, the question becomes, do we do theology? Our common authority may be the Bible, but whose interpretation, or exegesis, of the Bible is correct?

7

Systematic Theology and the Evangelical

Although there is much debate as to how theology should be done, there are certain rules that need to be followed – such as looking at the context of a passage, comparing Scripture with Scripture, examining the manuscript evidence and so on. This sort of study is called hermeneutics. When Christians take the study of God's word lightly and chisel random texts out of the Bible to build a structure, the resulting structure will not necessarily be the word of God.

And systematic theology, or the careful construction of a set of beliefs and doctrines from Scripture itself, is essential for this debate on unity. Systematic theology has been described as 'a discipline within the science of knowing God' because there is 'harmony and coherence' in this revelation.[45] A liberal theology, in contrast, seeks to harmonize Christian theology with the diverse elements of learning. Evangelicals base their understanding of what it means to be a Christian, what constitutes a church, how that local church is to be organized and how the ordinances are to be understood and administered on systematic theology. While there is, of course, diversity among evangelicals on their understanding of some of these points, they all argue their position from Scripture.

The strength of evangelical systematic theology is its demonstration of the interlinked, mutually dependent, revelation of the characteristics of God and his work that runs through the Bible. Though systematic theology cannot be by definition a 'science' in the empirical sense, it is a discipline for building a framework, a structure by which to know God. Systematic theology organizes the truths taught about God in the Scriptures thematically, and shows by careful correlation and exegesis how these truths are interrelated. P.T. Forsyth said that 'religion is an obedience before it is a liberty; and its first requisite is an authority'. For an evangelical, that authority is Scripture.

Yet no system, however structured and articulate, can itself be all the truth. Again, as Forsyth said, 'A theology, therefore, which is organized on a system of thought closed and self-contained can never be a due expression of that action, that revelation of a personal God, which creates religion; and certainly it cannot be its measure.' Yet without a systematic theology, he says, we have 'A religion of the free spirit without the fixed word' which is nebulous.[46]

Within their theological system, however, evangelicals have often appeared 'closed and self-contained' such that they have not been able to contribute meaningfully to the unity of the body of Christ. Any theological structure, including an evangelical systematic theology, can become a scaffolding – necessary and helpful, but a hindrance when its temporary nature of being a means to an end is misunderstood. Such a system can also become a theological strait-jacket. While a system offers security, fear that it will unravel completely can result if it is challenged. But when that system is based upon the truth, the word of God, and understood rightly as a means to obeying and glorifying God, any fear or insecurity should disappear.

Forsyth has highlighted yet another danger that has relevance for the unity debate. The result of systematic theology, he says, 'will inevitably reflect the cultural ethos of the community out of which the systematic theology has emerged and the issues before the church at any particular era'. The 'cultural ethos' of the conservative evangelical community is anti-ecumenical – in the modern meaning of ecumenical (a movement over the past century seeking visible and structured unity in the church). Both evangelical theology and practice reflect this ethos. And all of us, regardless of our theological views, are profoundly shaped by our foundational belief structures. I for one acknowledge that, as a conservative evangelical, it is difficult for me to step outside of the parameters set by my thinking or the thinking of our peer group.

But evangelicals have to come to terms with the fact that evangelical systematic theology emphasizes both the nature of the church as the people of the redeemed and its inherent unity. The present crisis of alienation and discord among the churches contradicts this teaching and so, regardless of the confusion and difficulty of the problem, evangelicals need urgently to confront it.

Some evangelical systematic theologians fear the domino effect. If they concede that the church is wider than their system, or that their dogmatics do not contain the whole, then they are vulnerable. How we define the nature and unity of the church depend on answers to such questions as the following: Who are the members? How are these members recognized? How does the church safeguard its 'purity'?

The foundation for the systematic theologian is the unity of the Godhead in redemption (Eph. 5:23), presuming a fundamental consistency in the outworking of God's plan of redemption in Christ. But unfortunately we cannot presume an equal consistency in the establishing and preserving of the church, the house and home of the redeemed. Christ's visible church, his body, is flawed and broken but, says Paul in essence, 'Christ is not divided even if you are' (1 Cor. 1:10). It cannot be right to leave the problem unaddressed.

We find the first rendering of this order of systematic theology in the creeds where, immediately following the great soteriological statement of God's work in salvation, is the statement of belief in 'the holy catholic church'. While 'church' is not foundational in the theologies of Strong and Berkhof, in Calvin's *Institutes* and right through the great Protestant confessions, the order is the same. The church has always been a pillar of the system for Calvin, Barth and others.

Theology is taught in Scripture and worked out in the church. Otherwise the Bible, if read in a vacuum, can teach anyone anything. Systematic theology is to be guarded – it can be a safeguard in itself as long as the system does not compress the truth. Comparing Scripture with Scripture is a legitimate and necessary exercise, but there must be room for mystery and apparent paradox. T.W.J. Morrow said, and I think correctly, that, 'It is however, interaction with the church catholic and a recognition of extra-biblical influences upon our formulations which will produce a more biblically balanced systematic theology.'[47]

Systematic theologies, no matter how carefully they are constructed, will always be fallible and coloured by the emphasis of their authors. Of the theologies that were particularly influential for me, it is common knowledge that Berkhof is Calvinistic, Hodge and Strong less so. Theology dare not be 'the product or the property of any single person, not even of any single sect or communion. It belongs to the Church as a whole', says Forsyth.[48] But no one theology can encompass the insights of all the churches, so all of us, from all different traditions, need to share our insights and convictions, evangelicals included. But where is the arena for evangelicals to share their insights? Not only is it unclear if there is an arena, but an apparent resolve on the part of some evangelicals not to share their insights at all, other than with themselves, creates further frustration, confusion – and division.[49]

Unless the teaching of the Bible is applied the theologian is 'little more than a kind of museum keeper who displays his ancient exhibits to the best possible advantage, but can do nothing to demonstrate their modern relevance', says Donald Guthrie in his *New Testament Theology*.[50] As theology is worked out in the church, part of the church's role is to bring checks and counter weights to bear upon it. Systematic theology is a necessary productive exercise. But if evangelicals are indeed handling truth, it cannot be a truth just for them. It is a truth that has to be brought to bear upon the church and be judged by the church. Evangelical truth is not only for evangelicals. Everyone would hesitate to name God as an 'evangelical' in the party sense. Theology needs the whole church if it is to approximate to the mind of Christ who is head of the church. The divisions in the church make its task immeasurably more difficult.

A divided church damages itself by contradicting the claims that it makes for itself. There is a credibility gap that everyone even remotely acquainted with the issues must appreciate. Newbigin says cogently,

> If the Church – or rather the 'Churches' – were a series of voluntary associations for the culture and practice of the religious life, their disunity might be deplorable but it would not be scandalous, and the problem of uniting them would be fundamentally a matter of mutual understanding and adjustment.[51]

Seeking for unity in that case would be an exercise not worth endeavouring to undertake because of the impossibility of the task.

But Newbigin is right when he states the problem in his book on the formation of the church of South India. The church is not a 'voluntary association'. If it were, the task and responsibility for creating interaction, whilst perhaps not simpler, would certainly be less pressing. Newbigin continues:

> It is true that both honesty and charity have compelled most of us to abandon the claim to be exclusively the Church, but that very abandonment has radically corrupted our church-manship, for it is very certain that the word ecclesia in the New Testament is an exclusive word, describing the body of Christ in the world, something of which it is unthinkable to predicate plurality except in the sense of the plurality of local Churches.[52]

The state of the churches is robbing them of what they were intended to be.

The church is to consist of people 'brought out of darkness and into light' (1 Pet. 2:9). It is the 'family of God' (Jn. 1:12). Today's disparate church would appear to be the antithesis of a 'gathered' church. A fractured church is robbed of one of its distinguishing features. Stephen Neill is correct when he says, 'It is unlikely that the unity of all Christians can be secured on the basis of inner and spiritual experience alone, without some form of outward expression.'[53] Only an outward expression of its unity can express for the church the claims it makes for itself. But how can evangelicals be a part of this? It is an important question, and the rather lame but unavoidable answer is that they are to begin amongst themselves.

In the following chapters we will take a tour through history to see how the missionary responsibility of the church has been one of the constant stimuli to press for unity. The unity of the church is never merely an academic exercise or even a theological one. In its present state, as one theologian has said, we as a church are 'nullifying our testimony'.[54]

A divided church causes as much confusion and is as much a hindrance to its mission as is false ecumenical thinking. There are echoes of Paul's teaching to the Corinthians on 'tongue speaking' here. If the 'world' hears from the church a babble of different 'tongues', it will think the church to be 'out of its mind'. But when 'everyone is prophesying' together, then the unbeliever 'will fall down and worship God' (1 Cor. 14:23–24). So many 'tongues' speaking different things confuse the world.

I remember well one "Morning Service" on BBC 4 in which the reading was from Acts 2. The reader commented that whatever else the Day of Pentecost was, it was about reversing the confusion of languages after the Tower of Babel. On the day the church was born, each heard the same gospel message in their own language. It was a 'type-ical' day, pointing forward to that time when people from every nation will together sing the praises of God with one voice around the throne (Rev. 7). The state of the church today is the antithesis of this wonderful picture.

So between the unity of Pentecost to the division of today … what happened? The answer will involve a little history. Time, space and context demand that we begin with the post-Reformation period and the rise of an evangelical contribution to ecumenical thinking.

III

How We Got Where We Are

8

The Rise and Fall of Evangelical Ecumenism

If we want to go forward we must ask how we got here in the first place. But take heart, for this is not your typical history lesson. The history of the church is dramatic and exciting – and enlightening. This history tells something of the hopes and disappointments, pain and frustration that belief in the unity of the church has engendered. And I hope I have given those who are truly interested some indication as to where to continue your reading.

We will look at the rise and fall of evangelicalism as an instrument for ecumenical endeavour. The uniting distinctives and characteristics of modern evangelicalism have been present from its very beginnings. So, too, have evangelicals always felt those pressures that pushed them towards separation – not only from the wider church, but among themselves as well.

Work by historians such as David Bebbington, in the area of evangelicalism, and Rouse and Neill in the field of ecumenism, has shown how evangelicals grew into a definable and recognizable part of the wider Christian church, transcending many of the barriers of religious and denominational life. This hesitant evangelical unity, despite the severe pressures to which it was subjected, grew into an

embryonic ecumenism from which the modern Ecumenical
Movement can discern its historic roots. That is not a matter of debate or embarrassment to evangelicals but rather
the story of its history. After looking at this history we will
explore how evangelicalism and the Ecumenical
Movement prepared the way for the antipathy that grew
between them after 1910 and is still, in large measure, with
us today.

So let's go back five hundred years or so. What happened to the church in the Reformation was the antithesis
of the word 'ecumenical' in its classic definition as 'world-
wide'. Yet there were those who, immediately after the
Reformation, became concerned for the unity of the church.
The tragedy of a divided church was apparent even then.

It may surprise some people that the first overture for the
church's healing was made movingly by Calvin himself, in
a letter to Thomas Cranmer, the Archbishop of Canterbury,
in 1552. John Stott quotes Calvin's letter:

> Doubtless it must be counted among the greatest misfor-
> tunes of our century that churches are thus separated from
> each other … and that the holy communion of the members
> of Christ, which many confess with their mouth, is only sin-
> cerely sought after by few. … From this it follows that the
> members being so scattered, the body of the church lies
> bleeding. This affects me so deeply, that, if anybody could
> see that I might be of any use, I should not hesitate to cross
> ten seas for this business, if that were needful …[55]

Other appeals in a similar spirit followed, although no-one
yet had a consciousness of a movement for church unity.
Richard Baxter (1615–91), who is rightly well regarded by
reformed Christians, was one of these early advocates for
healing the church. Baxter argued for principles for maintaining the peace of the church. He advocated avoiding the

following: 'controverted' opinions; stressing 'philosophi-cal' uncertainties or verbal controversies; items of faith that are not universally held or are new or non-Apostolic. In *The Reformed Pastor* Baxter displays his 'catholic spirit' – of which we will hear later – and even says, 'Of the multitude that say they are of the catholic Church, it is rare to meet with men of catholic spirit.' In speaking of the pains of a divided church he said, 'How rare is it to meet with a man that smarteth or bleedeth with the church's wounds, or sen-sibly taketh them to heart as his own, or that ever had solic-itous thoughts of a cure.'

But an embryonic pragmatic 'catholic spirit' would not be seen for another 40 years, and it would be longer still before there was a genuine seeking after a 'cure' for a bleed-ing church. It could be argued that, for evangelicals, this process began at the time of the conversion of John Wesley. When John Wesley's heart was 'strangely warmed', he was inadvertently helping to prepare the way for a unity that spread across the high walls of separation that existed at the time. It wasn't that Jews had no dealings with Samaritans, but the Christian had little contact with each other in differing streams of churchmanship.

Arnold Dallimore has demonstrated that Whitefield as well as Wesley had, like Baxter, spoken of a 'catholic spirit' issuing from a 'warmed heart'. Yet this 'spirit' did not take any tangible form for some time. Gradually, a common understanding of the gospel led to Christians recognizing like-minded people in other traditions. This took shape in the form of many practical initiatives based on a common theological emphasis, and the new Evangelical Movement was born.

For evangelicals, this self-awareness as an influential cross-denominational grouping became slowly apparent. As the Baptist historian Ernest Payne says that 'the evan-gelicals gradually won the day'.[56] But it would be a mistake to think of this in modern ecumenical terms – it was not so much a possibility for cross-denominational rapprochement as it was a self-recognition that crossed boundaries. And, as you might imagine, some of these boundaries were guarded by very high walls indeed. Joseph Milner, writing as long ago as 1810, could write of 'Evangelical religion, or what is often called Calvinism or Methodism'[57] – thereby linking the old and the new, and two theological and several denominational streams at one go, yet significantly linked by the word 'evangelical'.

Evangelicalism should still have this power to unite what many would think to be a separation; to bind together and embrace widely differing systems and histories around certain central truths. If Scripture is right, and evangelicals think that it is, then unity is a present and pressing evangelical responsibility as well as a mutual self-recognition.

Volumes could be written, and have been, on how the Enlightenment, Rationalist thinking and Romanticism affected evangelical attitudes and thought. The Romantic Movement, and its idea of 'personality', influenced the debate in a particular way, however. When John Wesley wrote, 'I judge it meet, right and my bounden duty to declare unto all … the glad tidings of salvation', this was not only a reflection of Wesley's Arminianism.[58] His idea, based on the concept that every human person has the 'right' to develop his or her own potential to the greatest possible extent, reflected the age in which he lived. It was his 'duty' to bring the liberation that the gospel offers to everyone – and that is not just a view of Romanticism but rather demonstrates obedience to the Great Commission, which is still required of us today.

This emphasis on the 'rights' of every person inevitably developed a social context. William Carey, the father of the modern missionary movement, in his significant 'Glorious

Door' address Enquiry into the *Obligations of Christians to use Means for Converting the Heathens*, 1792, writes not only of the call to preach the gospel in many places. He also saw an 'open door' that was opened 'by the spread of civil and religious liberty' and that 'a noble effort has been made to abolish the inhuman Slave Trade'. It was part of the 'activism' of which Bebbington writes. Ernest Payne writes of what was called 'vital godliness' linked to 'the age of societies' and how the Evangelical Revival 'found it possible to work together'.[59]

Evangelicals did not, of course, live in an intellectual or philosophical vacuum. There was mutuality and interaction that led to what Ken Hylson-Smith has described as 'pan-evangelicalism'.[60] The Methodist John Wesley was concerned with the evil of the slave trade, as was the Baptist William Carey and a whole gambit of this and other perceived evils were addressed by the activities of the mainly Anglican Clapham Sect. Evangelicalism then had a social dimension and a felt responsibility to reach out from beyond itself – as it should still.

But we need to look elsewhere to find a growing evangelical empathy towards an overt search for unity. Colonization abroad and industrialization at home both had a significant effect on moves towards unity. The founding of the interdenominational London Missionary Society (LMS) in 1795 was hailed as 'the funeral of bigotry'. On 9 May 1796, the LMS directors stated, 'It is declared to be a fundamental principle of the Missionary Society that our design is not to send Presbyterianism, Independency, Episcopacy or any other form of the church order and government ... but the glorious gospel of the Blessed God'.[61]

The missionary movement has always been foundational to the search for unity. In Calcutta, Baptist, Congregationalist and Anglican chaplains met frequently for united prayer. One of them wrote, 'As the shadow of bigotry never falls upon us here, we take council and go together to God's house as friends.'[62] William Carey, in a letter home to Dr Ryland, wrote, 'The utmost harmony prevails and a union of hearts unknown between persons of different denominations in England.'[63]

It was William Carey who proposed a Great Missionary Conference at the Cape of Good Hope in 1810. At the time Carey's conference idea was shrugged off as a 'pleasing dream', but the important point is that the dream had been dreamt at all. Though this sort of 'harmony' of which Carey spoke was little known in England, and despite the many factors militating against it, subsequently the EA was formed in 1846.

In order to fully appreciate the significance of the founding of the EA, it is vital to understand that it was formed at the nadir in Nonconformist/Anglican relationships, evangelical or otherwise. It is also crucial to be aware of other strains heightening the pressures towards disunity. As the former general director of the EA Clive Calver says, 'The most surprising thing about the birth of the EA in the first half of the nineteenth century is that it happened at all.'[64]

Barriers to evangelical unity

There were many significant hindrances to a demonstrable evangelical unity wider than the traditional barriers. We will look at just a few of these difficulties here. First of all, it will be a surprise to many that the rise of the Plymouth Brethren was such a hindrance to unity – especially as one of the finest statements on unity came from this group. Even as late as 1890, antipathy can be demonstrated. C.H. Spurgeon wrote in a letter recorded by Iain Murray, 'I cannot say that I have changed my opinion as to Brethren-ism; … their ideas of the ministry I do not accept'.[65] With due respect to the founder of my theological college, Spurgeon may have been ignorant of the comments of at least one of the early Brethren leaders who came right to the heart of the matter of unity.

I came across the following long extract from Roy Coad's *A History of the Brethren Movement* when recovering from flu (as one does). It made such a significant impression on me that I have endeavoured ever since to put into practice the principles it lays down. A.N. Groves, one of the fathers of Brethrenism who was concerned about where the separatist emphasis propounded by J.N. Darby would lead, wrote a letter to Brethren leaders and their congregations:

> Then what are these principals of Heavenly communion? Loving all whom Christ loves because they bear His impress; let this same rule then decide the question as to the subjects of our communion here on earth; all who Christ loves, who bear His impress, or whom we ourselves acknowledge as Christians. Should we ask how these are to be distinguished? We might hope that the Holy Ghost will help us here; but at all events, not so much by agreement in those points which are the subjects of intellectual perception, as those which are embraced by a hearty and generous affection towards the Father for his love; towards the Son, for His unspeakable self-sacrificing humiliation; and to the Holy Spirit, for His aid and helps along our arduous, tottering course, till we are presented faultless before the Son of Man, at his appearing.
>
> Should it be asked what are to be done with errors? Are they not a bar to communion? No; unless they bar Christ from the temple of the erring brother's heart. While we hope Christ lingers, let us linger: and rather be behind than before we quit, in pitiful remembrance of our own iniquities and unnumbered errors. So long as we judge Christ to be dwelling with a man, that is our warrant for receiving him;

and for the charity of that judgment that declares Him not there we are responsible.

The first duty to ourselves is in selecting the congregation with whom we should statedly worship; it should be the place where the form is most scriptural to our persuasion, and the ministrations most spiritual; where there is the sweet savour of Christ; where our own souls are most edified; where the Lord is most manifestly present with those who minister and those who hear. This is what we owe to the Lord, the church of God, and our own souls. Considering, however agreement in what we think best as to form of worship altogether secondary to heart-agreement in the mystery of Christ and godliness. These, then, appear the principles that ought to govern our selection, as individuals, of the places where we statedly worship, since personally we cannot be with all. Yet as to our liberty in Christ to worship with any congregation under heaven where He manifests Himself to bless and to save, can there be in any Christian mind to doubt? If my Lord should say to me, in any congregation of the almost unnumbered sections of the Church, 'What dost thou here?' I would reply, 'Seeing Thou wert here to save and sanctify, I felt it safe to be with Thee.' If He again said, as perhaps he may amongst most of us, 'Didst thou not see abominations here, an admixture of that which was unscriptural, and in some points error, at least in your judgement?' my answer would be, 'Yea, Lord, but I dared not call that place unholy where Thou wert present to bless, nor by refusing communion in worship reject those as unholy whom Thou hadst by Thy saving power evidently sanctified and set apart for Thine own …

To the question, 'Are we not countenancing error by this plan?' our answer is, that if we must appear to countenance error, or discountenance brotherly love, and the visible union of the Church of God, we prefer the former, hoping that our lives and our tongues may be allowed by the Lord so intelligibly speak that at last our righteousness shall be allowed to appear ... so long as Christ dwells in an individual, or walks in the midst of the congregation, blessing the ministrations to the conversion and edification of souls, we dare not denounce and formally withdraw from either, for fear of the awful sin of schism, of sin against Christ and His mystical body.[66]

Thinking not widely removed from that of Groves began to have an effect among evangelicals, but not in terms of structured initiatives for unity.

Initially, a common evangelical identity also worked against a need for a more structured demonstration of that unity. As L.C.B. Seaman says, 'Revived Christianity ... provided a popular culture and a deep emotional experience'.[67] These 'emotional', doctrinal and empathetic developments would have made such an idea for unity superfluous even if it had been formulated – which of course it never was!

Another reason for the lack of any coordinated ecumenical initiatives was the diverse nature of the Nonconformist churches. Right into the nineteenth century, Methodism in particular was forming several new connections. Evangelical self-preoccupation meant that the agenda was full and exciting and there seemed to be neither the need nor the desire for formulated unity initiatives. For Nonconformists this was still the age of striving for civil rights. The repeal of the Test and Corporation Acts in 1828 had been achieved in large measure from the stirrings of the Dissenters. Yet the battle for civil rights was to have a serious 'knock-on' effect in inter-church relationships.

In the winter of 1833–34 there was a remarkable upsurge of feeling among Dissenters that sought for the dis-establishment of the Church of England. No doubt the famous church historian Owen Chadwick is right when he says that 'During the early months of 1834 the discomfort between church and dissent thus reached a bitterness without precedent in English history.'[68]

The rise of the Tractarian, or Anglo-Catholic, Movement in Oxford from the 1830s deepened Dissenting fears even more. Yet, despite all of these barriers and many more, the EA was born into this time of great tension. It was described as a milestone in ecumenical history and has been fully recorded for those interested in researching the subject further.[69]

The Evangelical Alliance

Of the 800 delegates at the initial gathering of the EA in the Freemason's Hall, London (a venue that will raise a few eyebrows), ten per cent came from America and six per cent from the Continent, with fifty-two different denominations represented. Initial enthusiasm was boundless, with one delegate even suggesting that this was the 'beginning of the millennium'! The founding resolution is significant – it is probably the first modern ecumenical resolution. It read,

> The members of this Conference are deeply convinced of the desirableness of forming a Confederation on the basis of the great evangelical principles held in common by them, which may afford opportunity to members to the church of Christ of cultivating brotherly love, enjoying Christian intercourse, and promoting such other objects as they may hereafter agree to prosecute together; and they hereby proceed to form such a Confederation, under the name of the Evangelical Alliance.

Some of the pressures of any ecumenical dialogue, evangelical or otherwise, became apparent at once. Speaking of the drafting of the first EA resolutions, Dr Edward Steane, a Baptist minister and first secretary, said,

> It has required incessant thoughtfulness and the most
> watchful care lest an indiscreet word spoken or sentence
> written should wound the sensitiveness or offend the prej-
> udices of the curiously mixed and balanced ideas of which
> our association is composed – Churchmen and Dissenters,
> Presbyterians and Methodists, Establishmentarians and
> Voluntaries.[70]

Steane was the first drafter of modern ecumenical documents – most of which, it must be admitted, have produced
very little.

The ecumenical historian Ruth Rouse is in no doubt as to
the significance of the formation of the EA. 'But despite all
difficulties and obstacles, the reality of Christian unity had
at last found a corporate expression ... It was the one and
only definitely ecumenical organization which arose out of
the Evangelical Awakening in the nineteenth century.'[70] It is
clear that, in 1846, evangelicals were the first to see the need
to demonstrate the unity that they felt. But it was hard
work.

Both the tension and the success that accompanied the
first meeting of the EA in regards to evangelical unity could
be seen from the second day. The Anglican Reverend John
Jordan described his pain in removing a Baptist
schoolmistress, who he admired greatly, from his church
school because she could not conscientiously teach the
Church catechism. He also, nevertheless, told of how he
had invited a Wesleyan and a Baptist minister to 'a very
delightful meeting' which they anticipated repeating.[72] This
encapsulates the ecclesiastical climate into which the EA
was born – with its inbred, and to us often irrational, tensions. And yet it is also a unique expression of the sort of
Christian unity that the EA sought to encapsulate.

In the early years of the EA commentators have seen both
strengths and weaknesses. The organization stimulated

united prayer, especially in its week of prayer at the beginning of each year, and they took advantage of improved transportation and sponsored international conferences. The EA did sterling and pioneer work in the area of religious liberty, including representing and pressing for the rights of non-Protestant groups. One of the early slogans was that the EA 'made the invisible church visible'. That might sound corny now, but one must remember the religious climate into which it was born. Perhaps, with no formal thoughts of structured unity, the mid-nineteenth century was actually the high-water mark for evangelical influence and power.

The last fifty years of the nineteenth century saw many developments, including intellectual ones, that placed the entire church, evangelical or otherwise, under acute strain and drew the focus away from unity. When *Essays and Reviews* (1860) was published in Britain, many of the German views of 'higher criticism' were at first negatively received. But that stance changed within the main-line denominations, especially in their seats of learning, such that some evangelical scholars and the great commentators J.B. Lightfoot and B.F. Wescott saw it as a 'useful tool'.[73]

Scripture, as always, was central to evangelical debates, as in the 'Down Grade' Controversy of 1887–88 which beset the Baptists over perceived liberal trends in the denomination. This discussion mainly centred on the assimilation of 'higher criticism' thinking concerning Scripture amongst some. Although Ernest Payne could say that 'on the main theological issues raised by Spurgeon .... no schism took place',[74] Bebbington is undoubtedly correct when he writes that '"The Down Grade Controversy" helped prepare the way for sharper divisions among evangelicals in the following century'.[75] The evangelical attitude to Scripture had a far-reaching effect amongst evangelicals themselves and in terms of their relationships with others.

Another intellectual and theological development that affected evangelicals was premillennialism. Rather than looking forward to the triumphant return of Christ to set up his kingdom on a wave of gospel success, many, if not most, evangelicals now believed that Christ would first return to set up his thousand-year reign of peace and righteousness. Heralded by the 'great persecution' or tribulation, there would be a 'secret rapture' of the church. A key component of premillennial fervour was the imminence of Christ's second coming.

Premillennialism gave rise to new literature, societies and conferences, but it also meant that the church needed to change its agenda. One aspect of premillennial teaching was to describe the supposed dangers of a 'world church'. Rome was perceived as a threat to the true church, and Roman Catholicism was described as the Babylon of the book of Revelation, and the Pope as the antichrist. Evangelicals became overtly suspicious of anything or anyone outside their own constituency, which further separated them from the wider church. Not only did premillennialism affect evangelical confidence, but it had ecumenical implications as well. Evangelicals were moving far away from their roots, which were planted to grow, at least in part, unity.

There were some signs of a desire for more concrete expressions of Christian unity. One such indication was the Anglican Lambeth Conference of 1888. The conference drew up a statement entitled 'Lambeth Quadrilateral' for seeking a way forward. Although this policy has subsequently been amended, it has remained as the basis of Anglican ecumenical policy. Henry Lunn, 'a young Methodist of catholic outlook', organized the Grindelwald Conferences between 1892 and 1895 and brought together a range of churchmen ranging from Anglo-Catholics to Baptists. Not long after that, the Student Christian

Movement (SCM) and the YMCA provided some of the future leaders of the Ecumenical Movement, including John Mott and William Temple – two names that crop up constantly in ecumenical history. The age of the Ecumenical Movement was beginning to dawn, and evangelicalism was developing a more entrenched position against it.

The necessity for a pure church springing out of pre-millennialism led to an even stronger emphasis among evangelicals on individual salvation and personal holiness, expressed in books and conferences for the 'deepening of spiritual life'. Derek Tidball, principal of the London School of Theology, captures the atmosphere of the time well in his book *Who Are the Evangelicals?* 'Evangelicalism defined itself more and more in opposition to others and so brought its views of evangelical orthodoxy into increasingly sharper focus. Anti-ritualism, anti-Catholicism, and among Anglicans, anti-liberalism, became the key.'[76]

This was the age of the great evangelistic crusades designed, not to change the nation, but to save the individual. The great American evangelist D.L. Moody said, 'I look on this world as a wrecked vessel … This world is getting darker and darker; its ruin is coming nearer and nearer. If you have any friends on this wreck unsaved, you had better lose no time in getting them off.'[77]

The Keswick Convention, which was set up in 1875, had a wide-sweeping influence over the direction of evangelicalism. Under the banner 'All one in Christ Jesus' it confirmed the evangelical identity with its strong premillennial and eschatological emphasis. The teaching at Keswick emphasized holiness, victory over sin, witnessing and a deep personal experience of the Holy Spirit. Although according to the church historian Owen Chadwick, Keswick was at first disliked by evangelical leaders because of 'extravagances', the involvement of men like Handley

Moule, later bishop of Durham, helped to confirm and cement evangelicalism in its new direction.

Evangelicals were becoming introverted and, if they looked to the wider church, it was with growing suspicion. David Bebbington has observed that 'Evangelicalism, which had come so near to dominating the national culture at mid-century, was on the way to becoming an introverted subculture.'[78] This growing 'ghetto' mentality was to have far-reaching implications for evangelical relationships with the wider church and, particularly sadly, amongst themselves.

The First World Missionary Council at Edinburgh in 1910

New ecumenical initiatives during the twentieth century gathered momentum and evolved into a 'movement' from which most evangelicals increasingly distanced themselves, often with negative attitudes. One of the unfortunate spin-offs was a growing suspicion between evangelicals themselves which became more focused and concrete after the mid-1960s. How did this come about?

It would be difficult to underestimate the importance for ecumenicity of a council held in Edinburgh in 1910. The word 'ecumenical' entered into the general Christian vocabulary after this council, the First World Missionary Council. Certainly Edinburgh 1910 broke new ground in that the interdenominational representation included, for the first time, representatives from many Protestant traditions. It included evangelical missionary societies and, across the theological spectrum, the high-church Society for the Propagation of the Gospel. The agenda, to be addressed by such a diverse representation of churchmanship, could not but cause problems. Nevertheless, with mission as its title and theme, the council was consistent with the early 'ecumenical' stirrings epitomized by William Carey and others in the early days of the modern missionary movement.

Amongst others at the Edinburgh conference were the young William Temple, (future Archbishop of Canterbury and ecumenical catalyst), John Baillie (who would become professor of divinity at the University of Edinburgh and one of the original presidents of the WCC) and the ubiquitous John Mott. The spirit of the conference was enthusiastic and optimistic, yet theologically conservative. The preparatory commission confirmed this: 'But along with this generous recognition of all that is true and good in these [non-Christian] religions, there goes also the universal and emphatic witness of the absoluteness of the Christian faith.'

Even decades later, at the founding of the WCC, the verdict upon Edinburgh 1910 was eulogistic. According to Rouse, the ecumenical historian,

> It was a watershed between two eras of Church history. Before 1910 ecumenical movements were like rays of light struggling through a closed shutter into a dark room. Since 1910 the shutters have been flung back and light pours into all the corners of the room. There is 'a thousand times more aspiration, a thousand times more accomplishment.'[79]

As you can see, it is not only evangelicals who exaggerate! But for Rouse the council was exciting beyond measure as a major step in the history of ecumenism.

And yet, Edinburgh was not quite what some have thought it was. History has revealed that these massive international conferences would not bring about church unity in Britain – or anywhere else, for that matter. But even while the perception of Edinburgh's significance waned, its legacy lingered. For decisions and trends that came out of Edinburgh and were accentuated and crystallized in later ecumenical developments only served to increase the distrust that evangelicals felt towards the Ecumenical Movement.

A key negative factor for evangelicals was the basis on which invitations to attend the conference were given. While the council was made up of societies rather than churches, it was not open to all. 'Only those were included who were operating among non-Christian peoples. Efforts to win Christians from one form of the Faith to another – as by some American denominations on the continent of Europe, or among the ancient churches in the Near East, or among the Roman Catholics of Latin America – were not to be in the purview of the gathering', explained one commentator.[80] Edinburgh 1910 was attended, it was freely admitted, by those from a 'greater variety of ecclesiastical and theological convictions than had been represented in any previous gathering'.[81] This was bound to cause difficulties for evangelicals – and these difficulties were, as we shall discover, recognized even at the time.

The Sudan Interior Mission (SIM), which eventually grew to be the largest evangelical interdenominational missionary society working in Africa, was too small to be invited to Edinburgh. Yet the conference was initially greeted with warm anticipation by the mission's founder, Dr Rowland V. Bingham, whose initial view was typical of evangelicals. Writing in his mission magazine he said,

> The object of the great gathering is not to popularize the subject of mission but to draw together the world's experts ... No such effort has ever before been made by the church. The money will be spent in vain, man will toil in vain ... if we do not stand behind our leaders and pray down upon them the Spirit of God who alone can make the conference a true success.

But subsequently Bingham, while praising 'the unity and harmony that generally prevailed', was critical of the exclusion of those working in Roman Catholic countries and was concerned that 'the conference at Edinburgh seemed to aspire to a wider fellowship, and there were those who openly advocated the ultimate inclusion of the Church of Rome'[83] – a concept that was almost unthinkable then, and which is still problematical for many evangelicals today.

Bingham seemed able to perceive the way that ecumenism would develop from Edinburgh, as well as the long-term implications for evangelicals of excluding those societies working amongst Roman Catholics. He said, 'By the exclusion of the missionary work in South America from its reports and discussions the conference has forfeited its right to the term "ecumenical".'[84] It is interesting to note here that Bingham is still using the word 'ecumenical' in its classic sense of 'universal'. The word thereafter would refer, in the main, to an ecclesiastical 'movement'.

Despite Bingham's misgivings, the SIM magazine nevertheless published the entire findings of Edinburgh 1910. By 1911, however, a more considered critique was published. Bingham had heard Mott's opinion of the conference and especially noted his use of the word 'unity', which prompted Bingham to make three points (apparently the first statement of these views) that would dominate evangelical ecumenical concern for decades to come.

Bingham's first point pertained to the recognition of Rome as a sister church. His second was what he saw as the unfair representation of evangelical concerns. He said, 'Many missionaries wrote to the Edinburgh conference expressing these views [against biblical higher criticism] and giving their experience, and were astonished and indignant that their letters were not printed, while many others expressing the opposite views of the newer school, were found in the reports.'[85] His third criticism was the conference's silence concerning Satan. From the beginning of the modern ecumenical movement, typified by Edinburgh 1910, the Roman Catholic dimension and theological liberalism were problematical to the evangelical mind.

The conference in Edinburgh in 1910 did not end with the final benediction. A 'continuation committee' was formed, one of the members of which was our friend John Mott. This American Methodist layman had a gift for coining a phrase, including the following three: 'Evangelize to a finish and bring back the King', 'Bring Christ within the reach of every person in the world, so that he may have the opportunity of intelligently accepting Him as personal Saviour', and 'It is our duty to evangelise the world, because Christ has commanded it.' The modern church historian Adrian Hastings says, 'Mott represented very well the main American religious approach in these years – so far removed from the German – practical, optimistic, intellectually a bit naive.'[86] Even in his lifetime one historian could say, 'Mr Mott has an unrivalled gift of making the obvious sound really impressive.'[87] But he undoubtedly had something of significance to contribute, for, like William Temple, he crops up in the ecumenical story again and again. But Mott's slogans inadvertently make an important point. Words, however grand, however orthodox, will never deflect from ecumenical trends and evangelical concerns. This is a problem we will encounter again.

9

The Gulf Begins to Widen

Many evangelicals have felt a hard-edged antipathy to any-thing that smacked of the Ecumenical Movement – and this did not stem only from an obscurantist reaction to anything or anyone outside themselves. We need to understand the reasons for their animosity in order to make sense of some of the considerable negativism that was to follow.

Between Edinburgh 1910 and the Second World War there were three influential new ecumenical initiatives, and one old one (ecumenical now being used in its modern sense of a movement). These were the 'Faith and Order' movement, 'Life and Work', the International Missionary Conference and an *Appeal* stemming from the 1927 Lambeth Conference.

The *Appeal*

The Anglican Lambeth Conference in 1927 published an *Appeal to all Christian People* that moved the ecumenical agenda forward. It acknowledged that those who believe in Jesus Christ and have been baptized in the name of the Trinity share 'in the universal church of Christ which is His Body'. The *Appeal* concluded, 'we do not ask that any one communion should consent to be absorbed by another'.[88]

Ecumenical activity had moved a considerable way forward from Edinburgh 1910 in published intent and hope, if not in tangible result. In the 1920s the majority of evangelicals belonged to the main-line denominations. The strongly separatist groups had not yet fully crystallized, and only fifty years later would the many new congregations spring from the charismatic renewal.

The Lambeth Conference *Appeal* was problematic – not so much for evangelical sensitivities, but as it affected the historic Establishment/Free Church debate on issues such as church government and the historic episcopate. In the context of the Lambeth *Appeal*, the then Archbishop of Canterbury, Randall Davidson, paraphrased the 'high' and 'low' debate on the Anglican side – these words were not so descriptive of a theological position as they once were. One side was Catholic, certainly, the other not necessarily evangelical. Yet the debate at this stage primarily concerned churchmanship rather than doctrine (that would come later). Hence Ernest Payne, in *Free Churchman Unrepentant and Repentant*, would not have seen the debate in quasi-evangelical terms at all but in terms of the historic Nonconformist debate. In fact, in a comprehensive index to his book neither the word 'evangelical' nor its derivatives appear at all.

'Faith and Order'

'Faith and Order' and 'Life and Work' were two significant ecumenical initiatives that sprang from Edinburgh 1910 and were precursors of the WCC. The initial hopes of 'Faith and Order' were, from an evangelical perspective, exemplary:

> We believe that the time has now arrived when representatives of the whole family of Christ, led by the Holy Spirit,

may be willing to come together for consideration of questions of Faith and Order ... There is today among all
Christian people a growing desire for the fulfilment of our
Lord's prayer that all his disciples may be one; that the
world may believe that God sent him ... and that all
Christian Communions throughout the world which confess our Lord Jesus Christ as God and Saviour be asked to
unite with us in arranging for and conducting such a
Conference.[89]

The wording here seems unequivocally to eliminate the participation of Unitarians and was perfectly sincere in the
orthodoxy of its intentions. At the 'Faith and Order' conference in Lausanne in 1927 it is not the 'differences' that the
conference faced but their relevance to evangelical concerns
that is important for us – for they were prophetic of the problems that lay ahead. Many of the issues that would divide
evangelicals and the Ecumenical Movement subsequently
came to light at Lausanne. Conversations there revealed
great divisions concerning what the church was perceived to
be. William Temple saw the point immediately. Speaking
about the conference many years later, he recalled how the
'Lutherans and the Orthodox combined in a demand that we
must at all costs state concerning the church that it is both
visible and invisible'. Temple continued,

having first discovered this complete and enthusiastic verbal agreement between the Lutherans and the Orthodox we
then, as I say, regretfully added a footnote to say that they
meant not only different but diametrically opposite things
by it.

Temple makes perhaps the first overt reference to the perennial problem of ecumenism for evangelicals – namely that
people use the same words but understand them differently.

John Kent, the most recent biographer of William Temple, says, 'Faith and Order had always been a theological debating society whose discussions committed nobody.'[91] That would have little appeal for evangelicals, nor would it build their confidence in the ecumenical process. But I think we must be brave enough at this point to face a problem for evangelicals that comes up time and time again. When tensions do arise at conferences such as Lausanne, as inevitably they must, evangelicals can hardly complain that such matters as the nature of the church have been addressed and divisions have occurred. Evangelicals want it both ways. When there are apparently no differences, they say that they have been pushed under the carpet, and when differences are revealed they criticize the fact that there are differences.

I have often heard people say that the Ecumenical Movement is about compromise over essentials. Whereas many other evangelical criticisms may be valid, as we will see, this one is demonstrably false. For if the problem was compromise then it must be presumed that something tangible had been achieved in terms of unity by the Ecumenical Movement. But, other than empathy between differing Christian traditions (which is in itself no mean achievement), very little seems to have been achieved at all. In other words, people have not compromised. But no satisfaction is to be gained from that for, as the Anglican Bishop of Dornakil, India, put it succinctly at Lausanne, 'Divided Christendom is a source of weakness in the West: in non-Christian lands it is a sin and a stumbling block.'[92]

Another 'Faith and Order' conference was held in Edinburgh 1937. At all of these ecumenical conferences William Temple featured prominently – either by his presence, or rarely, in absentia. Because he was a master drafter of documents, Temple was able to paper over cracks. But by leaving matters unresolved he only stored up trouble for later. He was, despite opposition, the motivating force behind the formation of the WCC, and this time he brought up the 'sin' question.

In the 'Faith and Order' 1937 introductory sermon, Temple spoke of the divisions of the church as 'a sin'. If he was right, then the churches had no option but to address this 'sin'. But where the sin lies in a situation of division, and who is responsible for it, is always the moot point. A much-loved Christian leader, David Watson, who died too young humanly speaking, once described the Reformation as a sin – but not many would have agreed with him. If the Reformation itself was 'a sin' of schism, no party was going to confess it easily. Such matters will ever be coloured by the subjective viewpoint of the debater.

In this opening sermon William Temple said,

> We do not escape from sin by denying the consequences of our sin, and we cannot heal the breaches in the Church's outward unity by regarding them as unimportant. To those who made the breaches, the matters involved seemed worthy to die for.

As Temple says in his sermon, the Reformation issues cannot be dismissed as 'supplementary truths'. As David Hedegard, speaking from an ultra conservative position, points out that it is difficult to imagine what these 'supplementary truths' might be.[94]

Because of its place in history and the issues involved, there were no 'greys' in the theological spectrum at the time of the Reformation. It was black and white. Nevertheless, one suspects that a Luther or Calvin in any age would consider 'justification by faith alone' not as a 'supplementary truth' but as fundamental to the gospel. Evangelicals have never moved from this foundational doctrine of 'justification by faith', even as apparently the Roman Catholic Church has never officially moved from the *Decrees and*

Canons of the Council of Trent (sess. VI, can. II), which state: 'whosoever shall affirm that men are justified solely by the imputation of the righteousness of Christ, or remission of sin ... let him be accursed'. Clearly, when Temple or anyone else speaks of this kind of 'sin', it is going to be impossible to determine who is responsible.

When in the same sermon Temple said that he 'believed in a Holy Catholic Church, but could not yet see it', it is legitimate to ask whether he was using 'church' in a biblical sense. Apparently Temple was referring solely to the visible church and not to the wider or 'spiritual' concepts of the church. He was making one point as to the church's lack of visible unity. But he gave the impression that, for him, the only church was the visible one.

There was a heady optimism at Edinburgh 1937 that is not part of ecumenical thought today. The Report, for example, outlines the different concepts of church unity such as 'co-operative action', 'inter-communion' and 'corporate union'. While the Report does acknowledge 'co-operations' and the value of a 'federal' approach, it speaks much of 'organic union':

> In a church so united the ultimate loyalty of every member would be given to the whole body and not to any part of it. Its members would move freely from one part to another and find every privilege to membership open to them. The sacraments would be sacraments of the whole body. The ministry would be accepted by all as the ministry of the whole body.

That sounds good to me!

As these ecumenical conferences grappled with a multiplicity of intransigent and complex issues that divide Christendom, however, the evangelical could not help but see that basic truths concerning the nature of the church seem to have been forgotten amidst these other legitimate hopes and aspirations. While on the surface it could be argued that no 'doctrinal frontiers were crossed by the doctrinal Basis of the Faith and Order movement with the confession "Jesus Christ as God and Saviour"',[96] it was discovered that the formula could be interpreted in various ways – as was perhaps the intention. And here lies a root problem. Perhaps more than any other doctrine, evangelicals would be anxious that the 'Faith and Order' movement first understood the deity of Christ in its traditionally accepted biblical meaning, and then required acceptance of this belief for participating churches.

Theological liberalism was at its zenith during the interwar years. With the notable exception of William Temple – who in regard to the central truth of the deity of Christ was not liberal – many of the ecumenical leaders of the day were in the vanguard of this liberal trend. Temple contributed a section on 'The Divinity of Christ' to *Foundations: A Statement of Christian Belief in Terms of Modern Thought*. There were seven contributors to this volume and it was Temple's purpose, says commentator John Kent (drawing attention to *Foundations: A Statement of Christian Belief in Terms of Modern Thought*), to 'keep open a path to orthodox conclusions, protecting orthodoxy against the liberal passion for doctrinal redefinition'. But for several others, says Barry Till, it was not only on the ecumenical agenda that the debate 'had moved far ahead of anything the churches are likely to have reached'. They had moved on from orthodox theological norms in a whole raft of contentious areas.

Because of the Ecumenical Movement's drift away from central biblical truths, the evangelical perception of the movement became increasingly negative. If, as we have said, 'Faith and Order' had been merely a theological debating society, then there would have been little for anyone to be concerned about, evangelicals included. But 'Faith and Order' was a precursor of the WCC, the place where evangelical antipathy crystallized.

'Faith and Order', dealing as it did with 'authority' and the 'nature of the Church' – doctrines that closely overlapped and impinged upon evangelical theological sensitivities – could hardly be seen to be of merely passing significance. The other ecumenical dimension running parallel with 'Faith and Order' were the 'Life and Work' conferences, which were the most radical expressions of church and society yet and would eventually cause great problems for evangelicals.

'Life and Work'

The object of the Christian Conference on Life and Work in Stockholm, Sweden, August 19–30, 1925, is best described by the invitation to participants. It is quoted at length below to establish its *raison d'être*:

> We believe that there is a longing on the part, not merely of the trusted servants of the Church, but of all followers of our Lord and Master, to see Christendom so far united as to be able to work together in applying the principles taught by Him to the problems which confront us both in national and international life … No Christian can doubt that the world's greatest need is the Christian way of life, not merely in personal and social behaviour but in public action. The responsibility for helping to meet this need which rests upon all who name the Name of Christ cannot be exaggerated.

The document goes on to explain that the conference would not deal with matters of 'Faith and Order', but that rather 'a new impetus will be given to the various movements and strivings for reunion'. Yet the conference organizers were realistic enough to admit 'that we cannot afford to wait the fulfilment of that great hope of a reunited Christendom before putting our hearts and our hands to a united effort that God's will may be done on earth as in heaven'. In other words, the manifold needs of society should be addressed.

Not even evangelicals could quarrel with the conclusion of this invitation: 'We hope under the guidance of the Spirit of God, through the counsel of all, to be able to formulate programmes and devise means for making them effective, whereby the fatherhood of God and the brotherhood of all peoples will be more completely realized through the Church of Christ.' 'The world's greatest need', it went on to say, 'is the Christian way of life' – perhaps another way of saying, as an evangelical would, 'what the world needs is Christ'.

Although seeking to meet the needs of society might not seem a contentious set of objectives, some evangelicals did not believe that the church should intervene in these matters. This view was both a strength and a weakness. Derek Tidball, speaking of the same period as 'Life and Work', writes, 'Evangelicals betrayed their heritage and withdrew from any real meaningful social reform.' This withdrawal caused, he argues, the 'disastrous impression that Evangelicals have no social conscience or concern'.[98] But more serious reasons for concern were soon to reveal themselves.

The motto of the Swedish conference was 'Communion in Ecumenical Worship and Service'. All questions of faith and order were excluded from the agenda, on the apparently plausible if questionable basis that 'doctrine divides but service unites'. This phrase became one of the key expressions to focus evangelical negativism. Many of the issues of the time, such as the League of Nations, pacifism and the rising cloud in Germany, had an airing. But for many evangelicals this smacked of a social gospel.

The problem was that 'Life and Work' could never be what it was intended to be. It is doubtful if many British evangelicals at the time had ever heard of continental Christian leaders such as the Scandinavian Archbishop Soderblom. It was said at the time, 'It is impossible to exaggerate the part played in the conference by Archbishop Soderblom', but he was far from being an evangelical or even a doctrinal 'traditionalist'. From an evangelical standpoint, theologically he was a liberal.

At the following 'Life and Work' conference in Oxford 1937, which the German delegation was forbidden to attend, it became obvious that the questions as to the nature of the church could not be avoided any longer. 'As the work developed, the need for theological understanding came to be ever more strongly felt', record the ecumenical historians Rouse and Neill.[99] At the close of this conference a proposal was passed by an overwhelming margin for a World Council of Churches to be formed in which 'Faith and Order' and 'Life and Work' should become one.

Inevitably some, and not only evangelicals, felt that 'Life and Work' was 'influenced by the passion for identifying Christianity with Socialism'.[100] For A.C. Headlam, then the High and Orthodox Bishop of Chichester, the concern was not only socialism. In a letter to the Archbishop of Canterbury he expressed the fear that a WCC centred on Geneva might engender the 'habit of passing resolutions about political matters', so becoming 'even more futile and quite as provocative as the League of Nations'.[101]

The 'Life and Work' 'strand' was instrumental in the future direction of the WCC. Partly as a result of Temple's death, from 1948 onwards the WCC seemed to reflect more and more the 'Life and Work' agenda rather than that of 'Faith and Order', at least in its more publicized utterances. That perception would feed the negative attitude of evangelicals towards the Ecumenical Movement as represented by the WCC.

As we shall now see, the other strand of ecumenical endeavour that contributed to the formation of the WCC, the International Missionary Conference (IMC), also presented problems for evangelicals.

The International Missionary Conference

The International Missionary Conference was in existence before Edinburgh 1910 (in fact it called the council) and was not amalgamated into WCC until the 1950s. As Rouse and Neill point out, these were in the main 'Protestant' conferences and the nature of the gospel was not so much the issue as its 'dissemination around the world'. At Edinburgh 1910, apparently, the nature or the truth of the Christian message was not in debate, but rather its relationship to other world religions.[102] The 'matter of the message was relegated to the fourth place on the programme, and it was not the Christian message itself which was discussed but only its relation to heathen religions'. Nevertheless theological tensions were bound to appear afterwards between theological conservatives and liberals.

William Paton of the National Missionary Council of India became secretary to the IMC in 1927 and took up the organization of the follow-up conference to Edinburgh to be held in Jerusalem in 1928. This conference ran into difficulties over doctrinal tensions, for 'this was the hey-day of theological liberalism', says Barry Till candidly.[103] As a missionary statesman who was there put it:

> Some of the delegates put forward certain ideas which, if accepted, would have meant a revolution of the whole concept of Christian missions; the task of the missionary would

have been understood, not as trying to turn believers of other faiths into Christians, but as co-operating with them in the discovery of the riches of their own faith.[104]

At the conference, which was held on the Mount of Olives, the younger churches from the mission fields (mainly India and China) played an important part. A quarter of the 231 delegates came from such churches, many of them expressing 'the liberal point of view'.[105] Reflecting the concern of many of the delegates, and unlike Edinburgh 1910, a central part of the conference was devoted to 'The Christian Message'. William Temple was joint-chairman of the section on the Christian message in relation to other religions.

There is a dreadful familiarity about the format of the Jerusalem conference for those who, like me, have been to many such events. The mornings were spent in full conference and the afternoons in groups, after which the chairmen and secretaries drafted 'findings' to report back to the full conference. It was on these occasions that Temple's famous 'parlour trick', as he described it, was first brought into full play.[106] As the supreme drafter of conference reports, Temple was nearly always able to find a common denominator for a statement that everyone could agree upon at the end of the most diverse discussion. Temple is quite frank as to his methodology, which was 'fitting everybody's pet point into a coherent document when they thought they were contradicting one another'.[107] But such accommodation, of course, had to be at the cost of someone or something. Some of the theological impressions coming out of the Jerusalem conference could only be alarming to evangelical sensitivities.

Temple seems to have held a rather cynical view of himself and this ability. In the context of a relaxed, perhaps unguarded, letter to his wife on 4 April 1928, he wrote,

> I seem to have written what opens the doors for the pro-
> gressives while perfectly satisfying the conservatives ...
> There is great jubilation, as it is thought to be good in itself,
> and there is apparently great anxiety that we should not be
> able to agree on anything substantial at all.[108]

No-one would doubt Temple's personal integrity in this
matter, yet he is the personification of a fundamental problem that evangelicals have always had with ecumenical
statements. The evangelical suspects that there is an inherent theological weakness in seeking for a superficial agreement at the cost of truth, the lowest common denominator
rather than the historic faith.

As regards the content of the 'message' at Jerusalem, the
Chinese Professor T.C. Chao (who would later die at the
hands of the communists in China) gave a description that
appeared to be typical of the things being said:

> The Christian message lies clearly in the definite faith in
> God as Father, with whom his believing children can have
> personal communion with God through living of life as
> exemplified in Jesus, a life of moving and conquering love
> ... the love of God the Father, who wants all to be like
> Christ, and to have the most abundant life, that contains in
> it wonderful peace and joy and a contact with everlasting
> reality.[109]

That is hardly a statement of the 'message' as an evangelical would understand it. It contains nothing of personal
repentance or faith in the work of Christ on the cross.
Neither is another comment from Jerusalem, from another
Chinese delegate, helpful to evangelicals: 'Confucianism
contains all the essential ideas of Christianity except its idea
of God.'[110] This was further than the conference report was
willing to go, which said in an important statement:

Many of them had tried to find a synthesis of these two ways by saying that the Christian was one who had gone further along the same road that others were travelling ... Christianity was simply the higher climax of the same movement which they saw in all non-Christian religions; but that was not sufficient reason for missionary work. They could not demand such great sacrifices only to bring men a little further along the way which they were already travelling.

Another delegate, Dean M. Tarkkanen of Finland, gave the following evangelical reaction which supported the conference statement indicating that in the eyes of some there had been a move too far in the liberal direction. 'If anybody has received Christ, his Christianity will be much the same in Europe and Asia. To him who has found everlasting life in Christ, neither Buddhism nor Confucianism can give any new religious values.'[111] This was an evangelical's view expressed within the context of an ecumenical conference and one can but commend those who feel able to make such a contribution. Nevertheless, many of the evangelical interdenominational missionary societies either resigned from the IMC or never joined.

The third World Missionary Conference was held in Tambaram, South India, in 1938. Here the delegates from the younger churches outnumbered those from the West by 259 to 220. This conference does not seem to have made the impact of its two predecessors. What was the theological emphasis of the conference? It depends on your perspective. One conservative evangelical says that 'the theological emphasis was predominantly liberal',[112] while Till says, 'here conservatives were in the ascendancy'. When Till says 'conservative' he does not mean conservative evangelical, but rather the new 'conservatism' of Karl Barth.

T.C. Chao and H.W. Horton were prominent among the liberals at the conference. William Temple was not present.

The conference report, entitled *The Authority of Faith*, contained essays reacting to Kraemer. H.W. Horton wrote the following of a Buddhist priest he had met:

> If I belong in any sense to the Body of Christ, then he does, too. It would be blasphemy against the Holy Spirit, the Wind of God that bloweth where it listeth, for me to deny my Buddhist brother his place in that body. When I went to say as much to a group of Christians in Kobe the next day, I was sternly reminded that 'there is no other name under heaven given among men, whereby we must be saved'; but I thought to myself that I would rather have the Spirit without the Name, than the Name without the Spirit.

This statement is but one example of many revealing that by 1938 the third IMC had moved further still from an evangelical understanding of the gospel and its exclusive claims to the world.

Till emphasizes that the value of these conferences was they countered the danger of an academic theology was divorced from reality. They didn't draw the churches together so much as they produced an effect on the delegates in cross-fertilization that created Christian world statesmen. But by now evangelicals had little part in this 'cross-fertilization'.

With these three major strands of inter-church conferences the way was being prepared for the formation of the WCC which, but for the disastrous interruption of another World War, would have been formed earlier. Sadly, these conferences had also revealed many of the causes for future evangelical antipathy.

10

Preparing the Way

We have seen some of the foundational reasons for growing evangelical negativism towards the Ecumenical Movement. Not all of this aversion was a legitimate reaction to perceived liberal trends. Ernest Payne speaks of ecumenical negativism that comes 'largely from ignorance ... fanned in certain quarters by prejudice, misrepresentation and very questionable methods of controversy'.[114] Sadly that is ever the case with controversy and conspiracy theories. There was, nevertheless, plenty of reason for evangelical concern – as has and will be seen.

Foundations of the WCC

From 1937, the process leading to the formation of the WCC moved apace. When the Oxford 'Life and Work' conference ended, the delegates were joined in St Paul's Cathedral by those who were on their way to Edinburgh for 'Faith and Order', and the two 'could hardly stay apart much longer'.[115]

Despite the previous thirty years of ecumenical growth and activity it became obvious that, because of the overlap of personnel and agenda, a new initiative was needed. And so by the summer of 1937 the way forward for the

Ecumenical Movement had become clear. Although some expressed fears and misgivings, both the Oxford 'Life and Work' conference and the Edinburgh 'Faith and Order' conference voted strongly in favour of merging the two bodies.

Temple did much of the work to prepare the agenda, and a meeting was called at Utrecht in May 1938 where seventy churches were represented. At this meeting the future direction of the WCC was established, although it would be a decade before it finally came into existence. Here the draft constitution, the doctrinal basis and the scheme of membership were drawn up, although in theory everything had to be ratified by the member churches. Temple was appointed chairman of the Provisional Committee, with Visser't Hooft (a fine man who we will meet again) as its general secretary and William Paton (in London) and Henry Smith Leiper (in New York) as associate secretaries.

How much the evangelical voice was heard, if at all, would be difficult to ascertain. But in its early years the WCC seemed ignorant of, or unsympathetic to, that constituency. One of the reasons for this is that the ecumenical movement became introverted. John Huxtable puts it succinctly, 'Those who support and have been influenced by the Ecumenical Movement have a fellowship with one another which transcends denominational boundaries.' This 'fellowship' he sees as against 'Conservative Evangelicals' who believe 'fellowship presupposes theological agreement' and 'liberals who find themselves having much more in common with like-minded people in other communions than with the more "obscurantist" members of their own'.[116] Yet the lack of overt evangelical involvement meant that the movement was not representative of at least one important constituency.

After preliminary debate in 1938, the Anglican Church Assembly passed a resolution proposed by Temple on 11 June 1940, 'That this Assembly welcomes the establishment of the WCC constituted in accordance with the scheme sub-mitted to the Assembly and accepts the invitation to be rep-resented.'[117]

At the very height of the Second World War, another major ecumenical initiative was accomplished. The British Council of Churches (BCC) was set up in St Paul's Cathedral on 23 September 1942. The original membership consisted of sixteen denominations and several interde-nominational organizations, under the same doctrinal basis as the planned WCC. William Temple preached on this occasion – his influence seems to have pervaded everything ecumenical. Knowing more about William Temple himself will help us to understand some of the perceived strengths and weakness of the Ecumenical Movement, for they are reflected in him especially from an evangelical perspective.

William Temple

Temple's participation was paramount to the advance of ecumenism. There can be little doubt as to this great man's stance on theological fundamentals. 'I believe Christ walked on the water. I believe in the Virgin Birth', he said. If that note of Christian certainty and conviction seemed to be lost in future ecumenical perceptions, it was perhaps because of Temple's untimely death on 26 October 1944.

It could be argued that what evangelicals saw as Temple's weakness was that very quality that others believed to be his strength. Adrian Hastings writes on Temple's ecumenical involvement, 'The pope *in petto* was undoubtedly the ubiquitous Temple.'[118] His involvement in a countless number of cross-denominational and political issues, by no means all of them ecumenical, did not appeal to the average evangelical. Significantly in this respect, John Kent's biography of Temple pays comparatively little attention to Temple the ecumenist. He implies that, for Temple, ecumenism was not a primary concern but a compensation for other disappointments. He says, 'There was no question of personal failure ... but the [political] direction had changed: he had sidestepped the impasse of religion and politics and moved to the specialist area of ecumenism'. In this he is hardly correct, for Temple had been a steward at Edinburgh 1910 and had been present at almost every significant ecumenical event since. Temple the ecumenical specialist did have an effect on evangelicals, and his role and its spin-offs created some of the problems.

Perhaps there should have been more dissatisfaction with Temple's 'omnicompetence', as described by Hastings in a not altogether complimentary analysis of his ability to unite a gathering for a final statement.[119] It could be argued that Temple's organizing and drafting skills assisted the progression towards ecumenical bureaucracy, the route of the middle way, the accepted common ground, and the 'liberal' spirit. These were to bring ecumenism to a stony place which Temple could neither have envisaged nor desired, yet for which in some ways he prepared. Kent says that Temple 'differed from many of his evangelical and Anglo-Catholic contemporaries in his willingness to tolerate liberal theology at an official level'. These were, indeed, the two 'parties' that were to have the most difficulty with the Ecumenical Movement.

If the 'liberal-minded' Temple had stood unequivocally on his theological convictions in the ecumenical arena, then evangelicals might have participated more significantly in subsequent developments. Temple's death was a loss to the Ecumenical Movement and it could be argued that, had he lived, the movement would have been more theologically articulate. A lack of theological direction damaged evangelical/ecumenical relationships. Temple was no means unique among those involved in the Ecumenical Movement in holding these theological fundamentals, but evangelicals could be forgiven for thinking that these views were not seen as paramount in what Alan Gibson, a critic, calls 'comprehensive ecumenism'.[120] This mixed evangelical assessment of Temple mirrors the evangelical opinion of the Ecumenical Movement as a whole. Most evangelicals are either equivocal towards the movement of which he was a primary exponent, or unequivocal in their downright opposition.

The contribution of the BCC

The stated purpose of the BCC was to 'to act for the Churches in Britain in all matters of common concern relating to their participation in the worldwide activities of the World Council'.[121] It was this close link between the national and international bodies that was to colour the evangelical perception of the former when their antipathy towards the world body crystallized during the 1950s and 1960s.

Many evangelicals have presumed that the BCC was but a branch of the WCC and have tarred them with the same brush, under the general heading 'the Ecumenical Movement', but that will not quite do. Issues of church unity are too complex and diverse to be dismissed with such a catch-all phrase. Integrity demands that such a label, negatively loaded though it may be, should be assessed dispassionately. We always need to assess: what part or aspect of the 'movement' is being referred to? The evangelical constituency has become sensitive to words like 'charismatic', 'reformed' or 'fundamentalist' being used as negative catch-alls when each suggests a whole range of meanings and interpretations. So, in turn, evangelicals need to tread carefully, not damning everything under an umbrella as wide as the 'ecumenical movement'. But this widespread negativism is not without foundation.

The first post-war meeting of the Provisional Committee of the WCC took place in Geneva in 1946. After Temple's tragically early death, Dr Fisher, the new Archbishop of Canterbury, became the president of the BCC and took two rather surprising Anglican ecumenical initiatives, both of which were relevant for evangelicals. The first was addressed to the Free Churches, of which evangelicals were still a significant proportion. Fisher's second initiative was to commission a report from two Anglican groups representing the catholic and evangelical thinking in the church, called *Outline of a Reunion Scheme*.

These two groups were to 'consider whether any synthesis between Catholic and Protestant is possible'. The response of the evangelical group was entitled *The Fullness of Christ, the Churches' Growth into Catholicity*. One relevant clause on inter-communion states that what is required is not uniformity, even of doctrine, but 'that each believes the other to hold to the essentials of the Christian faith'. And, what is more, quoting from a report published a decade earlier, where there 'is corporate life in Christ' that common life should be 'demonstrated in the Lord's Supper' – hardly a radical idea today.

The word 'evangelical' no longer described one group of Christians in the church. Evangelicals were disseminating into new groupings such as the Fellowship of Independent Evangelical Churches (FIEC), with a new generation of evangelical leaders coming on the scene. Nevertheless, enough interest was shown by the Free Churches to appoint official delegates to take part in joint conversations as part of this project between 1947 and 1950. A final report, entitled *Church Relations in England*, was published. But, for evangelicals, 'constitutional union' was not now the main concern. Neither was church order primary. 'First and foremost there must be agreement on basic Christian doctrine (confessional) as an affirmation of scriptural truth, a preservative against error, and a unitive focus of church membership', wrote one Anglican.[122] For an evangelical this would hold as true now, if not more so, than it did then. By the 1950s the main sticking points to ecumenical progress were not the 'Orders' of the church but the essence of the gospel. Everything else was peripheral to the real issues, but as yet the main-line denominations were not expressing a strong negative reaction to the Ecumenical Movement.

11

The World Council of Churches

The ecumenical agenda for evangelicals would, from 1948 onwards, begin to shift radically. The first assembly of the WCC met in Amsterdam on 23 August 1948, a date which is now significant to only a few. At the time, commentators were confident that something of monumental importance was taking place:

> The 23 August 1948, will surely be remembered as one of the great days of modern church history. The constituting ceremony itself was very simple: a decision made by the assembled delegates, a minute of silence, and a Thanksgiving prayer by the Archbishop of Canterbury – that was all. But the event itself bore a weight of importance in church history. After centuries of isolation and division the Protestant and Greek Orthodox Churches had found each other and met in an attempt to share their common tasks.[123]

So why, you may ask, has the WCC become the source of such negative reactions and animosity amongst many? Originally there appeared little reason for evangelical concern in terms of the WCC's theological foundations. The 'Basis' of the WCC, as agreed in 1938, reads, 'The World Council of Churches is a fellowship of churches which accept our Lord Jesus Christ as Saviour and God.' There is no problem there, so why the worry?

The Basis

The WCC freely admits that it does not apply this Basis strictly, if at all, as a prerequisite for membership. The WCC states that its Basis 'is not a credal test to judge churches or persons'.[124] The Basis of the WCC is applied neither as a criterion for membership, nor as a ground for discipline amongst member churches. For, in the words of Till, 'it is the responsibility of each church to weigh its own acceptance of the formula. The only tests of membership applied by the Council itself are those of size and stability.'[125] How the churches interpret the Basis is their own affair. So it is blandly stated, 'Unitarians have been and are in membership.'[126]

A surprising source has defended the WCC's lack of action in implementing its Basis. The conservative theologian Klaas Runia noted not only that the 'Basis [was] sufficient for it is Christological, Trinitarian and about the Bible', but he also said that 'The WCC is not a church and therefore it has no right to act in a disciplinary way towards its member churches.'[127]

Nevertheless, the report of the first assembly expressed sentiments that were suitably and justifiably optimistic: 'Christ has made us his own, and he is not divided. Here at Amsterdam we have committed ourselves afresh to Him, and have covenanted with one another in constituting the W.C.C. We intend to stay together.'[128]

Even some WCC leaders, however, expressed concern at what they felt were weaknesses in maintaining the integrity of the 'Basis'. Bishop Eivind Berggrav of Norway, one of the six presidents of the WCC prior to the second assembly at Evanston 1954, proposed an amendment to the Basis. The text of his proposal read, 'The WCC is a fellowship of churches which, in accordance with Holy Scripture, confess our Lord Jesus Christ as God and Saviour.'[129] This proposal was at the time ruled out on the technical ground that it had not been sent to the constituent churches six months before the assembly met, as required by Article VIII of the constitution. Subsequently the central committee recommended that, at the third assembly, Article I of the constitution be altered to read, 'The WCC is a fellowship of Churches which confess the Lord Jesus Christ as God and Saviour according to the Scriptures, and therefore seek to fulfil together their common calling to the glory of the one God, Father, Son and Holy Spirit.' This new formulation of the Basis was adopted by a large majority at the third assembly: 383 delegates voted for it, thirty-six against, with 7 abstentions.

Although the new statement was more clearly Trinitarian, the new Basis was not going to be applied to anyone. If it had been, the Unitarians and liberals would have left. The new Basis remained open to interpretation. The Netherlands Reformed Church said that 'it would not attach too much importance to the new wording'. The Belgian Christian Missionary Church accepted 'in the hope that those Christian Churches which would not be able to accept or are not yet members of the WCC will not be disregarded or suspected for this reason', whilst the Remonstrant Brotherhood of the Netherlands trusted that 'the dogma of the Trinity may never become the touchstone of the admittance of churches'. And, lastly, the International Association of Liberal Christianity and Religious Freedom recorded that it 'deplores this action of the WCC which retards the advancement of religious co-operation'.[130]

For the evangelical, and in fact for any 'confessional' church, this ambiguity regarding the implementation of such a statement of faith is a major problem. By what criteria are theological words understood? How the Basis of the WCC is understood – by Scripture, tradition or free interpretation – must be ascertained if it is to have any meaning and purpose at all. Deliberate ambiguity, though an age-old device of which evangelicals are themselves past masters, should not be an alternative way of handling theological problems. G.E. Duffield, an Anglican evangelical ecumenist, rightly asked, 'is there a way forward by obtaining agreement on a certain basic minimum of doctrine covering the rule of faith, biblical authority the Gospel and the sacraments, by allowing conscience cases for minorities on biblical alternatives or non-essentials, and by leaving all other issues open?'[131] The trouble here is that Duffield's 'minimum' is hardly that if a statement even more minimal is not to be applied.

If the WCC Basis is not a 'test' but only to be 'weighed' and, if found wanting, to be sidelined or ignored, what is the point of having it at all? Here is one of the major reasons for evangelical antipathy to the WCC. The WCC is an organization to which churches apply with pre-knowledge of a statement of faith which, to ensure mutual confidence, integrity ought to cause to be binding .

Growing antipathy

In a set of essays produced in preparation for the first assembly in Amsterdam, the famous theologian Emil Brunner wrote, 'There has never been, nor will there be a Christian state or a Christian international order, but there ought to exist in every locality a Christian community imbued with the spirit of brotherhood and love.' This is, of course, right and makes demands on evangelicals as much as anyone else. Yet Brunner's 'ought' is prescribed by who and what constitutes the community of which he writes.

The early conferences of the WCC reflected its initial optimism. The theme of the Amsterdam Conference was 'Man's Disorder and God's Design' and emphasized a 'responsible society'. Evanston 1954 was generally agreed to be disappointing. The theme was 'Jesus Christ, the Hope of the World', but rather than hope being evident it was felt that 'the ecumenical honeymoon was over'.[132] The conference was not widely reported save for a comment by the Bishop of London to the effect that the WCC was 'a mixture of American money, Dutch bureaucracy and German theology'.[133] Perhaps even its own constituency was beginning to see the WCC as bureaucratic and following a self-motivated agenda. The WCC gained strength when it united with the International Missionary Council (IMC), which was a significant and logical move.

Up until now the IMC had been in fellowship with the WCC, but was not part of it. When the two bodies officially united at the New Delhi 1961 assembly of the WCC, many evangelical societies withdrew. Because of their pre-existing antipathy to the WCC, the amalgamation caused them to sever their connection with IMC. 'Many of these (missionary societies) were of a conservative evangelical – or fundamentalist – tradition, and as such they were suspicious of the WCC regarding it as "unsound" on questions of the authority and inerrancy of the Bible and, generally speaking, unscriptural and "liberal" in its theology', says David Bebbington.[134]

The next decade was to witness the very nadir of relationships between ecumenism and evangelicalism. 'The liberals and centrists together supplied the leadership in all the denominations except the smallest', Bebbington writes of the 1950s and 1960s,[135] and evangelicals felt isolated from the wider Christian scene. One prominent evangelical voiced the opinion of many: 'There are prominent elements in the WCC which do not want to make the movement all-embracing ... We are dealing with an active hostility on the part of a small but influential section of WCC leadership'.[136] There is a significant element of truth here, for certainly evangelical opinion was largely disregarded – as unfolding events were to confirm.

It was not only evangelicals who thought the third assembly of the WCC in New Delhi 1961 seemed idealistic. The report spoke of 'one apostolic faith preaching one gospel' and of the church

> having a corporate life, reaching out in witness and service to all and who at the same time are united with the whole Christian fellowship in all places and all ages in such wise that ministry and members are accepted by all, and that all can act and speak together as occasion requires for the task to which God calls his people.

This, of course, is pure 'ecumenese'. And it is not that this glorious state already exists, for the report blandly continues, 'It is for such a unity that we believe we must pray and work.'

Almost every word in the report, whether it be 'gospel', 'preaching' or 'ministry', is part of the problem of ecumenical understanding for evangelicals and others. Truisms heaped together sound almost platitudinous to anyone, and this sort of language compounds the ecumenical problem rather than helping to solve it. It is just not true, as the report proceeds to say, that 'We all confess that sinful self-will operates to keep us separated.' For genuine convictions separate as well.

One last 'Faith and Order' conference was held in Montreal in 1963, under the auspices of the Division of Studies of the WCC. Some described the conference as 'chaos' – even if some described it as 'promising chaos'. Here the Orthodox churches played a full part, as did Roman Catholic 'observers'.

John Mott began to perceive that the problem was a slide into an incipient syncretism, and at the end of his life he had 'grave reservations about a world body not motivated by mission'.[138] The general secretary of the WCC, Visser't Hooft (who evangelicals should reassess more positively), carried this concern further. He had been an ardent opponent of syncretism. In his book *No Other Name: The Choice between Syncretism and Christian Universalism,* he said that syncretism posed 'a far more dangerous challenge to the Christian Church than full-fledged atheism is ever likely to be.'[139] But for evangelicals an incipient syncretism was only a part of the worrying trends.

In a study on the theme 'Tradition and Traditions', it was accepted by the Montreal conference that 'we can say that we exist as Christians *sola traditione,* by tradition alone'. Barry Till says 'this was a donnish reference to the old Reformation war-cries that the Christian life could be lived *sola fide,* by faith alone, or that Christian truth is to be found *sola scriptura,* in the Bible alone' and was 'a significant move towards the Orthodox conception that the life of the church is the living tradition of Christ and the Apostles'.[140] If it was a move towards the Orthodox churches, then it was certainly also a move away from cherished evangelical theological norms. For, either way, to deny 'faith alone' or 'scripture alone', particularly for those of the 'reformed' tradition, was another nail in the coffin, and another example of the 'radicalism of the WCC' – to quote one opinion of many.[141]

The fourth assembly of the WCC was held in Uppsala 1968 and followed many of the themes taken over from Geneva. The conference followed the traditional pattern of apparently strong biblical affirmation with the theme

'Behold I make all things new'. If classic liberalism had already had its heyday, this was not evident at Uppsala. 'Even amongst convinced adherents of the WCC there was disappointment in the Assembly which seemed to be "a kind of theology-by-show-of-hands"'. That may sound like some reactionary fundamentalist opinion, but it is taken from the mandate of the Ecumenical Movement – *The Uppsala 1968 Report*, edited by Dr Visser't Hooft.

Another feature of the conference 'was its preoccupation – at times almost its obsession – with the revolutionary ferment of our time ... and with the most radical contemporary rebellions against all "establishments" civil and religious'. And that, too, was taken from the official report.

The chairman of the central committee of the WCC continued to develop this theme when he said the following year, 'the unity of mankind is the context and substance of the efforts of the Church to manifest its unity'. A special project was set up 'to enable the church to find its way in helping man to find his way'.[142] The ecumenical movement had moved a long way from Edinburgh 1910, William Temple, and the 'no other name' of Visser't Hooft, who had been retired but a few years.

The central committee, at a meeting in Canterbury in 1969, set up a programme to combat racism. That racism is an evil which Christians need to address and seek to combat was not the controversy. It was controversial that $200,000 was allocated to support organizations confronting racism, rather than to protest against the consequences of racism. The justification for this action was described in the usual high-sounding biblical and ecumenical sentiments which now strike a jarring note:

> Our programme is not against flesh and blood. It is against the principalities, against the powers of evil, against the deeply entrenched demonic forces of racial prejudice and

hatred that we must battle. Ours is a task of exorcism. The demons operate through our social, economic and political structures. But the root of the problem is as deep as human sin, and only God's love and man's dedicated response can eradicate it. The World Council's programme is but part of that response ... By God's love, by the power of his Holy Spirit, some day soon, we shall overcome.[143]

Regardless of the rights or wrongs of the action, the argument as it is stated here, in quasi religious journalese, must be unpalatable to most tastes. They anticipated trouble in the following press release:

The Executive Committee is well aware that some of the organisations supported are combating racism with violent means. However ... these organisations have given the assurance that they will not use these amounts received for military purposes, but for conscientization [sic], education and social welfare.[144]

In a now famous statement Pauline Webb, an English Methodist and a member of the executive committee, said,

The Fund must be seen to be a symbolic act – symbolic of a commitment that has very often been expressed by Christians ... but words have little effect until they become deeds ... the struggle against racism is not just a matter of charity or good-will, but it involves the transfer of power ... Inevitably, in some situations the struggle will involve the use of force. The Churches have never entirely denounced the use of force ... Now they are recognising, painfully and penitently, the possibility of 'the just revolution' ... In view of the fact that the majority of Christians are among the white, wealthy, powerful peoples of the world, it is surely not inappropriate that by this small symbolic act the World

Council of Churches might in penitence put a tiny balance-weight on the other side.[145]

The WCC had either never known or had forgotten William Temple's saying in his marvellous *Readings in St John* that 'whenever the Church picks up a sword, it cuts people's ears off'. This was certainly the case here, because the publicity that this initiative engendered meant that from this time on many, and not only evangelicals, turned away from structured ecumenism.

The new direction continued. A WCC conference on 'Salvation Today' in Bangkok in 1973 began,

> To call men to God's salvation in Jesus Christ ... to invite them to let themselves be constantly re-created in his image; in an eschatological community which is committed to man's struggle for liberation, unity, justice, peace and the fullness of life.

Whilst no word of itself might be untrue, the thrust and direction were obvious: salvation is in political and social transformation rather than in Christ, who make all things new.

The Nairobi Assembly of the WCC in 1975 continued in this overtly political vein. The section on 'Who Is this Jesus Christ who Frees and Unites?' reveals all of the current ecumenical emphases of the day. In one keynote address Dr Robert M. Brown, an American Presbyterian who was 'conscious of the sin of his own country' sprinkled 'buzz' words such as 'white guilt trip', 'tokens of solidarity', 'Jesus the Liberator', 'Marxism' and 'CIA' through his talk. Politically right-wing commentators began to perceive the WCC as Marxist and syncretistic.

And these commentators were not slow to promulgate this opinion. As recently as February 1993, a *Reader's Digest* article entitled 'The Gospel According to Marx' began with the question, 'Why have the interests of the World Council of Churches strayed so far afield from Christianity?' The director of the Programme to Combat Racism (PCR) is reported as saying 'the WCC concentrates on the "white institutional racism" of the "international capitalist economic system"'. If the *Reader's Digest's* figures are to be trusted, since 1970 the PCR has distributed over ten million dollars to more than 130 organizations in some 30 countries – about half to revolutionary Marxist movements in Africa. According to Rachel Tingle, director of London's Christian Studies Centre, 'The council has jettisoned traditional Christian missionary activity and substituted political action designed to establish a new kind of world order.'[146]

It seemed that the WCC either could not or would not try to understand the genuine concerns of its critics, including evangelicals. At Uppsala in 1968 the WCC linked 'fundamentalist' reaction to men like Carl McIntyre and Ian Paisley, who were hardly typical of main-line evangelical concern. But the WCC could not disguise the fact that evangelicals of all shades of opinion, in the main-line denominations as well as outside them, had become 'desperately concerned, if not disillusioned with the trends that had been indicated in the WCC', said Bebbington.[147]

Because of the fund to combat racism, in the 1970s there was debate within all the main-line denominations as to their ecumenical stance. Some evangelical denominations seceded, including the Salvation Army. By the end of this period from the 1960s through the 1980s, the gulf between the Ecumenical Movement and evangelicals had widened. One Van der Bent complained from a pro-ecumenical standpoint in 1974 'that there is hardly any critical literature on the ecumenical movement written from a constructive point of view'. He continues by being anything but constructive towards the ecumenical perceptions of evangelicals. He characterizes the conservative (evangelical) critique as 'being nothing more honourable than a smear campaign':[148]

> Most of these conservative Christians have at least a few ideas and concerns in common: individual conversion, adult baptism, the literal inspiration and infallibility of the Bible, an all-out opposition to liberalism and clericalism, a rejection of a 'super-church' and very often a seemingly neutral attitude towards political and social matters. Unfortunately all ultra-conservative churches and sects fail to realize that the universal message of their Lord Jesus Christ can neither be reserved for the conversion of individual souls nor be limited to the spotless life of a number of small Christian communities. If the Bible is commonly understood only by less than one per cent of all Christians, then surely something must be wrong with their 'correct' interpretation of the Scriptures.[149]

By this time, each side of the debate was caricaturing the position of the other. Both evangelicals and Ecumenists had an almost instant negative reaction to anything that referred to the other's perspectives.

The Ecumenical Movement had known both exciting and disappointing days. They failed to bring about church unity. Kenneth Slack, one of the foremost ecumenical leaders, wrote a little book in 1960 called *The British Churches Today*. When he revised it in 1969 he discovered that 'passage after passage of the book written in 1960 has seemed strangely optimistic and has had to be excised'.[150] By the mid 1970s the unity talks between Anglicans and Methodists had failed, and the early ecumenical optimism seemed to have evaporated.

During the heady days around the time of the Second World War, Temple could describe the ecumenical movement by saying 'a great world-fellowship has arisen; it is the great new fact of our era' and of a 'deeper unity – an actual experience of Christian fellowship across all secular divisions which is full of hope for the future of Christendom and through it for mankind'.[151] But by the end of the 1970s political decisions, as well as a perceived theological emphasis, brought the WCC into a steady decline in influence. 'Temple's vision of a single Christian ideological movement ... had been lost', was the opinion of Temple's most recent biographer – and time has proved him correct.[152]

To add to the WCC's problems, confidence, international co-operation and self-awareness was growing within the various denominational structures themselves. Instead of churches looking outward to their responsibility for ecumenical initiatives, they were increasingly caught up with their own place within the world-wide church, and this was to be particularly seen amongst evangelicals who were growing, if not yet rapidly in numbers, then certainly in self-awareness.

The 1950s in Britain saw the major Billy Graham crusades, interdenominational conferences such as Keswick were at their zenith, and there was, as Derek Tidball points out, a new sense of self-identification and confidence. Evangelicals saw little need for, or purpose in, ecumenical structures. They were about their own agenda, even if they were still given little credence by much of the ecclesiastical establishment who were, almost by definition, ecumenically committed.[153]

The formation of a World Evangelical Fellowship, a World Congress convened by Billy Graham in Berlin 1966, and the Lausanne Movement which called an International Congress in 1974, meant that evangelicals were speaking to each other. At the same time, strong voices were speaking out against ecumenism, and fears and phobias were being broadcast and published around the world. People were identified more and more with their own constituency, and they became nervous of offending it.

Strong evangelical leaders, such as Martyn Lloyd-Jones of Westminster Chapel, London, were drawing around them groups of ministers and leaders who found their identity in their constituency rather than in the wider church. Such groups as the Westminster Fellowship, Banner of Truth, and British Evangelical Council (BEC) were articulately anti-ecumenical. Antipathy to ecumenism bound evangelicals together – but that was soon to change.

12

Developments in Main-line Churches from the 1960s

If a week is a long time in politics, three decades can bring immense changes in the life of the church. A visit to one of the main-line evangelical churches at the beginning of the 1950s and again in the 1970s would reveal differences almost impossible to describe. If this chapter, which is more of a general overview than a detailed study, seems to major on Anglicans and Baptists it is because they are the constituencies best known to the author. But what is true of these is also true in measure of other main-line denominations. Although evangelicals had long been a 'party' within Anglicanism, by the 1950s things were at a low ebb. Alister McGrath, in his biography of J.I. Packer, says,

> After the Second World War, evangelicalism was in a sorry state in England. It had lost its position of power it had once had in the national church. It was numerically weak. It was treated with something like contempt by academics, especially academic theologians. It was dominated by forms of Pietism which stressed the importance of personal intimacy with Jesus, yet discounted as an irrelevance any serious thinking or engagement with theological issues.[154]

By the mid-1970s it became evident that the main-line denominations had a changing perception of evangelicals. In the 1950s and early 1960s three significant books were published among many that raised the evangelical profile and increased evangelical confidence. The first was *The New Bible Dictionary*, a project begun in 1953 and not published until 1962, J.I. Packer's *'Fundamentalism' and the Word of God* in 1958, and John Stott's Basic Christianity (published earlier in the decade but reissued as a paperback in 1957).

With the introduction of family communions and the gradual demise of matins and evensong, Anglican church life took on a markedly different pattern. Changes, such as new liturgical forms and worship styles, increased lay participation and less formal clerical dress, all meant that the evangelical Anglican world was no longer so predictable or easily identifiable by outward forms.

Also, the 'unholy alliance' between evangelicals and Anglo-Catholics that had brought down the Anglican/Methodist unity plans was renewed to react against liberal bishops such as the then Bishop of Durham, David Jenkins, and to enter into debates on such topics as the ordination of women. Evangelicals and Anglo-Catholics shared many fundamental truths and, though the source of their 'authority' was somewhat different, they were not the enemies that most had always presumed they were. The secular media began to seek the High Church for a response to matters of the faith. The Anglo-Catholic Archdeacon of York, George Austin, rather than the evangelical Archbishop of Canterbury, George Carey, was the representative and spokesman to the media for orthodoxy through the 1990s.

Some of the perceptions that were to influence evangelical Anglicans also affected Baptists. The Baptists had always had a stronger evangelical constituency, as well as less structured ties to their denominational bodies. Some of the more conservative Baptist ministers and churches left the Union after Martyn Lloyd-Jones' call for separation from the main-line mixed denominations in 1966. Still more left in 1971 after one of their theological college principals, Michael Taylor, appeared to deny the deity of Christ in an assembly address. Although the cries of dismay and anguish were loud and clear, the majority of the evangelical constituency remained in the denomination. Those who did secede had the strongest antipathy towards the Ecumenical Movement and became identified with the separatist form of evangelical independency.

After these secessions, the continuing evangelicals were either committed to their denomination, its structures and ecumenical stance, or were so busy with their own agenda of maintaining the life and witness of the local church that what happened elsewhere seemed irrelevant. Baptists, like the evangelical Anglicans, did not suffer numerical decline to the same extent as the other denominations.

In the other main-line denominations, Anglican and Baptist evangelicals were increasingly being identified as having a similar agenda. Anglicans and Baptists had worked together in the evangelistic initiatives of the 1980s. Both were strongly represented in pan-evangelical organizations and at events such as the EA and Spring Harvest. Both were deeply affected by the Charismatic Movement.

Believer's baptism, previously one of the greatest causes of separation between two of the most active groups of evangelicals in the country, was no longer quite the issue that it once was. A substantial number of Baptist churches did not insist on believer's baptism as a prerequisite for membership, nor did Anglican churches bar those in good standing with other churches from communion. Through ecumenical projects (Local Ecumenical Projects [LEPS]) a few joint Baptist–Anglican churches were formed.

All of this led to a new 'ecumenical' cross-fertilization among these two groups of evangelicals. In the new climate where the mutually held distinctives of evangelicals – such as biblical preaching, evangelism, and latterly charismatic influences in worship – were evident, there was a free movement of worshippers between churches. People still held to certain tenets of distinctive belief but subjected these to what was considered to be more essential. Many evangelicals would find their church home to be that which best suited their ethos and emphasis, with little regard either to that church's denominational title or to the tradition in which they had been brought up. This was by definition being 'ecumenical', even if it was not recognized as such. Sensitivities to historical affiliation and the search for a 'pure' church had become primarily the concern of separatists.

In an oblique way, the Charismatic Movement played a part in the changed ecumenical outlook of evangelicals in general. Even in main-line evangelical churches not specifically involved with the Charismatic Movement, the structure of worship had changed significantly. Many of the separatists who retained their theological distinctives, being 'reformed' in the sense of Calvinistic, were little influenced by charismatic trends. Separatist churches guarded their memberships by teaching on the dangers of outside influences. Warnings were, wisely, given on the perils of compromising the truth. In matters of polity, in seeking to ensure a 'converted' membership, and even in a 'closed' communion table reserved for baptized believers, separatists maintained their distinctives with little cross-fertilization with churches of other traditions. They also stood apart from, and were invariably hostile towards, the new charismatic 'phenomena'. The form of their worship adapted more slowly and they were hesitant to take part in joint ventures where they would be exposed to charismatic teaching and experiences other than a few songs.

Separatist evangelicals were becoming ever more separate, preoccupied with their own distinctives and peers. In the main-line evangelical subconscious there was a growing awareness that they were not the only people of God. Evangelicals in the independent traditions began to wonder, sometimes not without reason, if the ecumenically 'compromised' churches in the denominations were in fact evangelicals at all.

By now the divide between denominational evangelicals and separatists was so wide that there was little contact between ministers or their churches. Historic conferences like Keswick, although its perceived holiness teaching was still held in suspicion by many on the Reformed wing, continued to attract evangelicals from both wings – though fewer separatists would attend than previously. While independent ministers met in evangelical ministers' fraternals, main-line evangelical ministers met in denominational groups or local ecumenical fraternals. The days of Martyn Lloyd-Jones, when seceders from the main denominations joined the independents in some numbers, had passed. Attitudes expressed by separatists were unlikely to attract evangelicals from within main-line groupings and there were far more evangelical ministers within the denominations. The evangelical missionary societies were still the main bridge between the two groups.

Adrian Hastings said that the position of evangelical Anglicans was now 'very moderately sacramentalist, socially committed, biblically conservative but not obscurantically fundamentalist, cautiously ecumenical'. Of evangelicals in general he said,

> It may, however, well be the case that in England there remains no real alternative for evangelicalism between an intellectually archaic and fundamentalist sectarianism on the one hand and absorption as a Conservative and biblically

conscious wing within an ecumenical Catholicism upon the other.[155]

This is a more contentious and less accurate opinion. The majority of evangelicals, 'growing towards fifty per cent of Protestant church attenders in the United Kingdom', according to Clive Calver, understand themselves to represent neither an 'intellectually archaic fundamentalism' nor a 'wing within an ecumenical Catholicism'.[156] These alternatives are too black and white. Nevertheless, the evangelical's dilemma is to understand his position within the wider church, while the separatist is wrongly dismissed as being 'sectarian' and of no consequence. How can a mainline evangelical remain in structures apparently leading in directions that he does not wish to travel, without being compromised in his basic convictions? And how can the convinced yet hesitant separatist not slide into fundamentalism and obscurity with others who have travelled that path before? As we shall see below in Chapter 15, Swanwick 1987 brought all of these questions to the fore. But first let's turn to the unravelling of the intervening years.

13

1966 and All That

There are historical and theological reasons for some separatist negativism towards anything that smacks of ecumenism. Let me make two things clear. Firstly, when I use the words 'separatist' or 'separatism', I am not using them in any derogatory sense at all. They describe those who are inherently opposed to ecumenism, and I still have many friends amongst this group of people.

In a strictly English context, 'Nonconformists', as independent of the state, or churches 'Free' from the establishment, date back almost to the Reformation, and historically all Nonconformist or Free churches are, in that sense, separatists. Later independent chapels and churches were formed that were 'separate' from any of the now-established Nonconformist denominations. Many of these churches were to form or became part of the FIEC. There are also, of course, a host of independent churches including Pentecostals, Grace Baptists, Independent Baptists, Continuing Congregationalists and many others. By and large they would not want to be linked with the umbrella word 'ecumenism'. It is in this sense that the word 'separatism' is being used here – 'anti-ecumenical' in the modern sense, post-dating Edinburgh 1910.

There is also a difference between 'independence' and 'separatism'. For example, many of the new charismatic churches are independent but not necessarily anti-ecu-menical. There are many Christian leaders who come from independent backgrounds but who would not think themselves to be 'separatist' in the sense described here. The reasons for separatist ecumenical concerns and fears, many of them wholly legitimate, need to be examined.

Perhaps the first specific act of evangelical 'separation' in this modern sense took place in the student world. The Cambridge Inter-Collegiate Christian Union (CICCU), along with other Christian unions, resigned from the Student Christian Movement (SCM) in 1910 over its perceived liberal theological stance. CICCU joined with these other Christian unions to form the Inter-Varsity Fellowship of Evangelicals Union (IVF), which would later become the Universities and Colleges Christian Fellowship (UCCF).

But it is to a more recent time that we must look. One result of the increasing sense of alienation felt by evangelicals towards the Ecumenical Movement was a sad division among themselves. During the heady ecumenical days of the 1960s such as Nottingham 1964, there seemed to be little regard for evangelical sensitivities, yet at the same time evangelicals were themselves becoming fragmented as never before. One of the main causes was, again, ecumenism. For by the mid-1960s church unity was also on the evangelical agenda. In the brief description of events that follow I would stress two things. The perception of what happened is coloured by the prism through which each looks at the events. For those who would read further, the separatist evangelical understanding is mapped out fully in Iain Murray's biography of Martyn Lloyd-Jones.[157] For an understanding of the events described and the consequences that followed from the main-line perspective, Alister McGrath's biography of James I. Packer is of particular interest.[158]

In 1965, the EA formed a Commission on Unity as an outcome of an EA National Assembly held the same year.

Unwittingly, this constructive move was to have the effect of fracturing evangelical unity to such an extent that, as yet, there has been little healing, or sign of it.

The crisis sprang from another EA assembly held the following year, in 1966, and centred on two evangelical giants of the time: Martyn Lloyd-Jones, the minister of Westminster Chapel; and John Stott, rector of All Souls, Langham Place, whose ecumenical sympathies I have indicated. We need to understand what happened here for three reasons. First, it had seminal impact at the time; second, it had far-reaching consequences (which I lived through as a very young theological student at the time); and third, without an appreciation of these events it is difficult to fully understand the subsequent history of evangelicalism and the Ecumenical Movement, which we will examine in the chapters to follow.

Much of separatism focused over the next 30 years on the first of these men, the late Martyn Lloyd-Jones. In his address to the opening rally of the 1966 National Assembly of Evangelicals he said,

'I would dare to suggest tonight that we find ourselves in a new situation. And the new situation has very largely been caused by the rising and revival amongst us of what is known as the Ecumenical Movement, which began in 1910, but has become a pressing problem to us as Evangelicals, especially since 1948.' He continued, 'The denominations throughout the world were now prepared to put everything into the melting pot in order that a new world Church might come out of it.'[159]

That this new 'world church' has never shown any sign of emerging has not lessened the impact that Lloyd-Jones made at the time, or the influence that he has since had on those of like mind. Neither was his viewpoint wholly negative.

Peter Lewis, an independent minister from Nottingham, says that Lloyd-Jones had argued for some time 'for the need for a closer and more visible *evangelical* unity as distinct from the *ecumenical* unity that was being strongly pushed in the church at large, and of which he was critical'.[160] Iain Murray, Lloyd-Jones' official biographer, summarizes his argument as follows:

> He differed with ecumenism on its fundamental principle namely, that all dialogue should proceed on the understanding that it was between fellow Christians. He objected to this because it meant giving a breadth to the meaning of 'Christian' which was unknown in the New Testament . . . Certainly he believed that a man might be a Christian who did not employ the name 'Evangelical' . . . But the fundamentals of evangelicalism are the fundamentals of the gospel and to concede the title 'Christian' to those who deny those fundamentals is to undermine Christianity itself.[161]

Lewis further endorses this view, saying that Lloyd-Jones argued that, 'Instead of simply adopting delaying tactics in their denominations, Evangelicals should themselves take up the New Testament emphasis on unity.' In fact, Lewis continues, Lloyd-Jones 'saw no hope for evangelicalism in the ecumenical movement, or in the mixed denominations, since he believed it would inevitably be compromised and watered down in its essential "gospel" character.'[162]

Gilbert Kirby, the EA general secretary at the time, explains the context of the momentous assembly in 1966. He says that at the previous assembly in 1965, 'the question of Christian Unity was uppermost in many minds,' especially in the light of a Commission on Church Unity. Many of the leading evangelicals of the day either were members of this commission or contributed to it.

This commission had came to the conclusion that there was no widespread demand to set up a United Evangelical

Church. Rather, there was a need to strengthen links between 'evangelical churches of varying traditions, with an effective fellowship or federation between evangelical churches both locally and nationally'.[163] Before the now-famous Anglican Keele conference of 1967, ecumenical attitudes were not so clear-cut as they are today. Yet, in both the main-line denominations and separatist congregations, ecumenism was a general concern. Within a few years all this was to change, and many have held 1966 to be a turning point.

To blame Lloyd-Jones for personally wrecking the serene waters through which evangelicalism seemed to be sailing at that time of the 1966 assembly, just at the time when evangelical self-consciousness and confidence were rising, would not be fair. It cannot justifiably be argued that Lloyd-Jones abused the platform that the EA National Assembly had offered him on 18 October 1966. The Rev A. Morgan Derham, general secretary of the EA, writes in the foreword to a book of the papers given at the assembly,

> At the Public Rally on the evening before the Assembly proper, the main speaker was Dr D. Martyn Lloyd-Jones of Westminster Chapel, who had put his views personally to the Commission; the members of the Commission, knowing that this was a viewpoint which others Evangelicals share, *had asked that he should state it in public* at the evening meeting, which he did.

Lloyd-Jones had both a right to his view and the right to express it by responding to an invitation given him. He was not directly responsible for what followed, although his address was to have disastrous consequences for evangelical unity.

Immediately after Lloyd-Jones spoke, John Stott publicly dissociated himself from what had been said. In the opinion of some commentators, Stott spoke improperly. Perhaps he overstepped his authority as chairman, in light of the fact that Lloyd-Jones had been invited to speak as he did. Stott said, 'I believe history is against what Dr Lloyd-Jones has said ... Scripture is against him, the remnant was within the church not outside it. I hope no-one will act precipitately.'[165] The result by all accounts was 'sensational' and 'polarised' the meeting.[166]

The outcome of these events is freely admitted. 'One immediate consequence was a deep division both between Anglican Evangelicals and many of their non-conformist brethren, but also among non-conformist pastors and churches.'[167] But it would be wrong to infer that the meeting itself caused the division, for it had already begun. One writer says of that evening, 'I went to the Central Hall that night, disillusioned with the Baptist Union, desiring closer unity with Evangelicals.'[168] The reason for this disillusionment was, no doubt, the ecumenical issue. The writer, then a Baptist Union minister, reveals his thinking when he says,

> In most of the doctrinally mixed denominations, Evangelicals were, at best, marginalised and ignored, but often mocked and discriminated against. Many young, evangelical ministers were fighting for survival, and would often find that a denominational official was working in league with disaffected members, to get them out of their churches. Numerous good, evangelical, theological students, looking for a church, were passed over. The Ecumenical Movement was marching forward to conquer, with strident voice and big steps, but with little sympathy for those who stood in the way.[169]

This statement seems to make two things clear. First, it indicates something of the siege mentality of certain evangelicals at the time. The writer was in a denomination where the majority were evangelicals. The 'conspiracy' overtones he directed towards the denominational heads were not, apparently, the experience described by other evangelical ministers. Yet it must be freely conceded that evangelicals were not strongly represented in positions of influence in the structures of the main-line denominations at the time. Secondly, the author, writing 30 years after the event, reveals that little has changed in the thinking of many separatists since the momentous events of the evening of 18 October 1966, save that ecumenical attitudes have further hardened. Why should this be?

Certainly the evangelical agenda since 1966 has been mainly in the hands of mainstream evangelicals and the rapidly emerging charismatics. Perhaps a ghetto mentality has grown amongst separatists. James Packer, according to McGrath, 'was one of the few evangelicals to advocate continued collaboration with Free Church evangelicals after the showdown of 1966'.[170]

Another, and more likely cause, for these attitudes was the death of Lloyd-Jones. In him the separatist constituency had a leader of considerable ability and influence. Lloyd-Jones was recognized by evangelicals representing positions much wider than any one constituency, and he has never been replaced. The separatists agree: 'One obvious difference between 1966 and 1996 [the 30-year anniversary of the events described above] is the figure of Dr Lloyd-Jones ... Our greatest weakness is a lack of an awakening ministry in the nation',[171] said Geoffrey Thomas – and this sadly is undoubtedly true as much in 2007 as it was in 1996.

Lloyd-Jones had lost influence in wider evangelical circles even prior to his death. Sir Fred Catherwood who, as Lloyd-Jones' son-in law and a deacon of Westminster Chapel at the time is more qualified to speak of him than anyone, has written of the Doctor's 'passionate plea for

Evangelical unity', to which he added this sad postscript on the outcome of 1966. 'Evangelicals divided instead of uniting. In retrospect it is easy to say that he should have left it there. But the vocal minority, who wanted to translate his plea into a united Evangelical Church, also wanted him as their leader, and he was identified with them and was lost to the Evangelical majority.'[172]

One of the results of the 18 October 1966 debacle and succeeding events has been that, sadly, separatists have become increasingly distanced from the wider evangelical stream of influence. They are in danger of being perceived as a single-agenda party as anti-ecumenists. This is not true.

But there needs to be a significant change in mindsets all round. Evangelicals in the main-line churches seem often, in my experience, to ignore the splendid contribution that those from separatist traditions can and should be making. But there are reasons for this, too. Many evangelicals know little of the work that separatists are doing and do not know their leaders at all. This is a considerable weakness.

We have seen that the Ecumenical Movement has engendered legitimate concerns. Yet it could be argued that these concerns have given rise to negativism towards anything not clearly recognizable as being of the one constituency. Packer himself was cut out of the Puritan Conference, of which he had been co-founder, and excluded from the *Evangelical Magazine*, of which he was co-editor. It is difficult to underestimate the effect of the events of 1966 on two continuing streams of evangelical Christians who moved inexorably apart.

Most Christians worshiping in separatist churches rejoice in the strengths that the constituency provides. But among some there is a negative sentiment which stems from a few hard-line leaders. There is a fear from within the constituency that some pastors and leaders have to face.

What will others think? What will be the effect of stepping 'out of line'? Such thinking is the fruit of marginalization. A leader or organization that needs to look constantly over their own shoulder is unlikely to make inroads into a wider agenda.

For separatists, the fear of ecumenism grew out of all proportion. Significantly, Geoffrey Thomas, one of the constituency's most articulate spokesmen, wrote of 1966, 'Perhaps that was one weakness of evangelical beliefs in 1966 – they gave more credence to the power of the Ecumenical Movement than it merited.' Subsequent events have proved that opinion to be true. The Ecumenical Movement has not had the power or influence that was attributed to it by its critics.

Alan Morrison's book, which has been given much credence by some and is significantly called *The Trojan Horse: The Hidden Agenda of the Ecumenical Movement*, said,

> The hidden agenda of the Ecumenical-Interfaith Movement will one day be exposed for all to see – a movement which plays a major role in the satanic strategy designed to destroy the unique witness of the Christian Gospel. For with their "Super-church" they are bringing in the earthly kingdom of Antichrist.[174]

All of that sounds a little passé now. Jack Hoad writing a history of Baptists from a decidedly separatist standpoint says, 'The Union [Baptist] has endeavoured to recover an "evangelical" appearance.'[175] It seems that he cannot concede that the BU might not have an evangelical gloss but *be* evangelical. Hoad states that the reason for Baptist 'decline' is an ecumenical one. What is not mentioned is the reason why the constituent churches from which Hoad writes have known more rapid decline by far than the Baptist churches of which he is so critical. The great news concerning the

Baptists in Britain and the Presbyterian Church in Ireland is that denominations can be brought back to their evangelical roots when ministers and leaders are committed to that recovery. The spiritual decline so obvious in the UK has nothing to do with the events of 1966 – of which people in general have never heard. But people are aware of the divisions in the church.

I have sought to demonstrate that, for the evangelical, there were real problems in the Ecumenical Movement. Even the general secretary of the WCC wrote of the acute danger of syncretism. Nevertheless, time has revealed that the fears of the past are not to pervade the demands of the present. Those demands are so pressing as to preclude anything that denies our unity in Christ.

If it could be presumed from what I have written that for separatists anti-ecumenism was the all-pervading agenda, that would not be true. They are gospel churches about their gospel work. Nevertheless, the fruit of 1966 has been disastrous for British evangelicalism. The BEC has been replaced by Affinity. Affinity must and will make concerted efforts, if not to inaugurate a change of stance towards ecumenical contact, then certainly to become increasingly in touch with the whole gambit of evangelical Christians operating outside of the main-line denominations. And it must not end there. As revealed truth comes increasingly under attack, the time has come when evangelicals from all constituencies must stand together.

14

The End of the Ecumenical Movement?

If we ask why evangelicals are hostile to the Ecumenical Movement we also have to ask why, for many years, the Ecumenical Movement was hostile to evangelicals. 'Evangelicals in the 1950s felt the pain of assault. It was clear that they were despised and rejected and dismissed out of hand, particular on account of their high view of Scripture.'[176] For some decades after the war, ecumenists did not seek evangelical contributions. J.D. Douglas, former editor of the *Church of England Newspaper* and British editorial director of *Christianity Today* reported that the atmosphere was hostile towards evangelicals at the first British Faith and Order Conference in Nottingham in September 1964. Perhaps not surprisingly, evangelicals became increasingly introverted and focused on their own agendas. Even in articulate evangelical circles,[171] the response to ecumenism was at best ambiguous and at worst hostile.

Ambiguity and hostility

As Derek Tidball notes wistfully:

> The ecumenical movement, I believe, needs to show a greater understanding of the evangelical perspective and to appreciate that its concern for truth is not to be regarded as secondary to the concern for unity but must run parallel with it. Likewise, it would do well to appreciate the alternative ecumenism of evangelicalism rather than denigrate it.[178]

Understanding grows from building relationships, and it is a two-way process.

When denominational evangelicals such as Baptists and Anglicans did come into positions of influence that demanded it, they too became ecumenically involved. They could not represent their constituencies without contact with other denominational leaders. Often, due to suspicion or other priorities, evangelicals have not been as committed to their denominational structures. Baptists and independents emphasize 'the autonomy of the local church', which should 'be respected by those who represent the churches', says Andrew Green.[179] But it was the denominational response to new ecumenical initiatives that caused many main-line evangelical churches finally to examine what was taking place. From 1966 onwards, 'the existing aversion of the Baptist Revival Fellowship (BRF) to the ecumenical movement' was reinforced, says David Bebbington.[180] At that time the BRF represented a considerable constituency within the Baptist denomination.

But by that time the gulf between evangelicals inside and outside of the denominations had grown considerably. By 1971, for example, all but one of the officers of the BRF had seceded from the Baptist Union (BU). There was little contact between evangelicals who had always kept themselves apart from the ecumenical process and denominational evangelicals. They not feel a natural rapport and the feeling was mutual.

The denominational position of many evangelicals is an expression of their view of the church. The separatist Alan Gibson expressed the thoughts of many when he wrote the following:

> If we regard this [the denomination] merely as historical tradition, denomination is evidently expendable. If, however, for us, denomination reflects biblical norms of doctrine and polity, we shall rightly be jealous to guard it. This will not necessarily mean unbending rigidity on our part, but it will certainly not lead us to throw out a denomination or its label unthinkingly in favour of para-church co-operation.[181]

While in the 1960s, in Bebbington's words, 'The standard view [of evangelicals] was that external uniformity was unimportant and that there were risks in being too involved in the quest for reunion', evangelicals now began to move in opposite directions and some were changing their attitudes to the Ecumenical Movement. The negativism of Separatists and independents merely became more entrenched. Increased Roman Catholic ecumenical involvement confirmed the gradual move back to Rome that they had always suspected.

One ultra-Protestant writer, Michael de Semlyen, saw an unholy alliance between charismatics and Roman Catholics at work:

> Like other 'para-church' groups which led the charismatic movement in the '50s and '60s, the FGBMFI (Full Gospel Businessmen's Fellowship International) brought Roman Catholics and Protestants together in the 'unity

and love of the Spirit', placing emphasis on experimental testimony rather than on scripture. Controversy was to be avoided; difficulties that arose over doctrine, discouraged.[182]

As the title of his book confirms, for him *All Roads Lead to Rome.*

The view of one Roman Catholic ecumenist, John M. Todd, would have confirmed the belief of the ultra-Protestants had they read the following,

> ...the trend is undeniable. Many of the doctrines which were once anathema are gradually creeping back into acceptance. And with them come the Catholic practices ... It is not for Catholics to look scornfully on these developments, but to be thankful for the steps which are being taken slowly but surely back to the norm, and to see in them the preparation of these bodies by God for their eventual return to full communion.[183]

And Todd was no Catholic eccentric but went on to co-found the Roman Catholic ecumenical publishing house Darton Longman & Todd. As to what 'full communion' means, he said,

> Any return, corporate or individual, must involve recognition of the Pope as the vice-regent of Christ. Once an individual has reached the point of recognising this truth, he cannot stay outside Catholic unity, since he would in that case be refusing obedience to Christ in the person of his earthly vicar.[184]

Here was the sort of confirmation of Roman Catholic attitudes that many separatists were looking for. And they found it, paradoxically, in their Catholic counterparts.

Changing Baptist views

Many evangelicals within the denominations held views on the Ecumenical Movement that were quite similar to separatists. In 1939 Baptist evangelicals had seen ecumenical involvement as unimportant and inconsequential, then in the 1950s they acknowledged that it allowed their denominational leaders to have wider roles, and finally came to hold a firmly negative view in the 1960s and 1970s. Ernest Payne, one-time general secretary of the BU, had been elected a vice-president of the WCC at Uppsala and is described by Hastings as the most committed ecumenist his time.[185]

Baptists had been members of the WCC from the beginning. In his history of the BU, Ernest Payne says that 'the Baptist Union had accepted the invitation to join in 1939'.[186] When a growing negativism to the WCC began to materialize, the Baptists maintained their affiliation partly out of the fear of losing their place as a significant player in the wider denominational world and partly out of regard for Payne's standing and influence, 'despite some disquiet'.

Separatist Baptists have strongly criticized this policy of affiliation. Jack Hoad, a Strict Baptist now Grace Baptist, writes from this separatist standpoint in *The Baptist* that 'The failure of the Baptist Union churches throughout this long period of doctrinal decline is highlighted by a study of their failure to protest effectively against the successive actions of their leaders.' And again,

> There has prevailed a 'stay-in-to-win-it' philosophy which is characteristically non-Baptist. In chronicling the spiritual decline of the Baptist Union, there is no comfort to be found in doing an unpleasant task from the knowledge that there are many evangelical churches still to be found who have not bowed the knee to Baal.[187]

Even if this is a caricature of the situation pertaining to the BU, it is true that pressure from evangelicals began to mount. By 1974, because of the WCC's socio-political agenda, pressure was brought upon the BU to withdraw from the WCC.

But things were to change. Although there was organized opposition to BU participation in Churches Together in England (CTE) after the Baptist assembly in Leicester in April 1989, continuing membership was ratified at Plymouth 1995 by an 'overwhelming' margin with a 90.21 per cent vote in favour.

So why the change of thinking? It has to be admitted that through the 1960s and 1970s, with the exception of the formation of the United Reformed Church (which in itself created division within the Congregational denomination), the Ecumenical Movement had failed to make the progress towards unity. After the ecumenical zenith of Nottingham 1964, according to Hastings 'the most important British ecumenical conference ever to be held',[188] it was all downhill. A resolution for visible unity had been passed in 1964, with a target date of 1980. That may sound ridiculous now, but perhaps it did then as well. Norman Goodall wrote later of 'The splendidly irrational symbol of the date "1980"', but it is a classic example of the heady ecumenical thinking of the time.[189]

The theme of the Nottingham conference was 'One Church Renewed for Mission', and on the final day they passed the following resolution:

> United in our urgent desire for One Church Renewed for Mission, this Conference invites the member churches of the British Council of Churches, in appropriate groupings such as nations, to covenant together to work and pray for the inauguration of union by a date agreed amongst them.

> We dare to hope that this date should not be later than Easter Day, 1980. We believe that we should offer obedience to God in a commitment as decisive as this.

Till describes the Nottingham conference as one of the two high-water marks of BCC activity. Not only was 1980 to come and go with no sign of this unity, but the BCC itself would no longer exist as such by the end of that decade.

The failure of Methodist/Anglican negotiations

Throughout the early 1970s the Methodist/Anglican reunion negotiations had dragged on and were eventually unsuccessful. 'We offer ourselves wholly to thee, asking that thou wilt renew in us thy blessing already given, and that thou wilt transcend the differences of our calling and make us one by bestowing upon us what thou knowest us to need for thy service as Bishops/Presbyters in thy universal church and in the coming together of the Church of England and the Methodist Church'.[190]

Quite clearly, for the evangelical and the Anglo-Catholic, neither was quite sure what was going on, whether this was historic episcopal ordination or not. Both united against it for opposite reasons. The evangelicals feared that what they hoped was not happening might be, and the Anglo-Catholics sensed that what they thought was essential to happen, might not be happening!

Structured ecumenical schemes had been failing for over a generation, and Hastings writes of a 'progressive course of depression through the collapse of institutions of renewal and the fading away of its leaders'.[191]

Barry Till, a committed ecumenical historian, felt the pain of the failure of the Anglican/Methodist union negotiations. Here is an illustration of how an evangelical, or anyone with strong convictions, can be a serious frustration to those seeking a middle way. The matter was lost, Till says, because the evangelical and the Anglo-Catholic viewpoints were completely different:

> In this vote the Church of England found itself between Scylla and Charybdis. Neither extreme party was able to accept the view that a totally logical and water-tight solution was in the circumstances impossible. Neither was able to feel that in the over-riding interest of the unity of the church the application of the principle of 'economy' might be possible.

This principle of 'economy' is rarely open to the evangelical in any matter, however, let alone the ecumenical debate. The whole appeal of Till's book is that evangelicals might explain their position firmly and graciously within the debate – not from the outside where only misunderstanding and resentment arises. Till is essentially right when he says that,

> The Methodist vote is in one sense a vote about the nature of the Church of England. Not for the first time at a moment of crisis the tail is wagging the dog. In this case it is a Siamese tail. In the last century the two parties [evangelical/Anglo-Catholic] came together to resist intellectual change in the face of Darwinism, Biblical criticism and the like. In 1969 they came together again to reject the change which may be thought to be most typical of – and necessary to – the church of the twentieth century.[193]

The anger here is as intense as a reputable scholar can be in print. But because they cause anger it does not mean that convictions are to be jettisoned for the sake of a superficial peace.

The failure of the Anglican/Methodist unity proposals was a serious blow to the prospects for 'institutional' ecumenism. Time was to prove that neither 'Covenanting for

Unity' nor the 'Ten Propositions' – two more ecumenical initiatives of the 1990s – would be successful. In the words of Lesslie Newbigin, 'the whole movement which had begun with the Lambeth appeal of 1920 seemed to have come to a dead end', due to 'the lamentable fading of the ecumenical vision in the minds of English church people'.[194] But it had not come to a dead end in the minds of its critics.

Ecumenical plans and schemes followed each other apace, but they met limited success and growing antipathy from evangelicals. As one separatist says of ecumenism, 'The biblical gospel is not denied, it is by-passed as being irrelevant, even divisive', and 'It will be those who remain true to Scripture in the ordering of church relationships who will be regarded as heretics'.[195] The BEC was a constant and principled opponent of the whole ecumenical process, particularly of evangelicals in the 'mixed denominations'.

Yet not only evangelicals felt this way. Grass-roots support for ecumenism was low. 'Schemes', 'covenants' and 'propositions' did not motivate people in the pews. When the General Synod of the Church of England rejected the covenanting scheme enshrined in the 'Ten Propositions' in 1982, Hastings said that the 'last hope of a national way forward within a Protestant framework was abandoned'.[196]

The church directed its energy elsewhere. The activists, who were not confined to the traditional evangelicals, were interested in doing rather than debating. In the 1980s Billy Graham's 'Mission England' drew people together from many different denominational backgrounds in an evangelistic initiative. In comparison the endless ecumenical round 'seemed to have become an irrelevance and rather a boring one too', said Hastings.[197]

The Ecumenical Movement had 'run out of steam'. It had failed not only by evangelical criteria, but by its own as well. By the time of the Swanwick conference in 1987, the movement was ready and brave enough for a change of direction.

15

Swanwick 1987

Churches together ... or churches apart?

By the end of the 1980s a vibrant and confident 'main-line' evangelicalism had little time or interest in formal ecumenical activity. EA, under the leadership of Clive Calver, was at its most active, Spring Harvest had become a force to be reckoned with, and the Charismatic Movement was making striking headway. But significant ecumenical developments that would have an impact on evangelicals, at least on those within the main-line denominations, were taking place.

The Swanwick conference, held from 31 August to 4 September 1987, paved the way for a significant change of direction in the British ecumenical scene, and on 31 August 1990 the BCC ceased to be. The new initiative was at first called 'Not Strangers but Pilgrims' and then 'Churches Together' (in some areas 'Christians Together).

Although we have seen the failures of the Ecumenical Movement from the mid-1960s onward in terms of achieving the goal of visible unity, there were positive changes in ecumenical attitudes. Almost without realizing it, many evangelicals altered their stance in regard to ecumenism in ways that would once have been impossible to imagine. This attitude shift deepened the division amongst evangelicals themselves, however, and left a chasm in some ways wider than that between evangelicals and non-evangelicals.

Douglas McBain, former general superintendent of the BU for London and an evangelical and charismatic, said, 'We have been active participants in the great contemporary adventure of ecumenical relationships'.[198] An evangelical Anglican, Canon Michael Saward, wrote of 'the uneasy relationship between separatists and Anglicans who are evangelicals' and continued, 'I suspect that we simply live in different worlds.'[199] Many separatists would agree.

That church unity *per se*, or a united church (either nationally or locally) would impress the non-Christian to such an extent that it would draw him or her to that church has never been proven. Perhaps it never could be. This is a particular area of evangelical sensitivity, for it touches on the question 'What is the gospel?' It is primarily independent charismatic and Afro-Caribbean churches that have seen the greatest numerical growth.[200] Ecumenism, however worthy a cause, was not the vehicle for winning the world for Christ that Mott had hoped it would be. Nevertheless, it did foster a mutual if unstructured recognition among main-line churches.

For Christians began to develop fresh perceptions of one another. Visser't Hooft recognized this when he said that 'The traditional differences between the denominations continue to exist. But they are crossed by trans-denominational dividing lines ... and [people] stand on the same side as people from another denomination.'[201] This is particularly true of evangelicals. As honorary president of the WCC Visser't Hooft recognized the implications of this. 'Is it possible for the churches to have ecumenical relationships with each other, while they are struggling with deep divisions among their own members? What is the point of conversations between churches where there is hardly a church which can say that it represents one single particular theological position?' he bravely asked.[202]

And so formal ecumenical structures grew increasingly irrelevant. The Ecumenical Movement in Britain had accelerated after the war. Many evangelicals within the mainline denominations, though indirectly involved through their denominational structures, watched from a distance. The marginalization of evangelicals was often, but not always, their own responsibility. Due to apathy, or antipathy, or because they were too busy with their own agendas, they had little influence upon proposed structures for unity decided by their denominational leaders on their behalf. But irregardless of structures, attitudes would change slowly.

By the time of the 1987 Swanwick conference sponsored by the BCC, the paths of the two groups of evangelicals – independents and those in denominations – had diverged widely, and the Swanwick Declaration did nothing to bridge the gap. Denominational leaders represented their evangelical constituencies at the conference, but no separatist leader would have dreamt of being present at a BCC conference – his convictions would not have allowed it and his constituency would not have tolerated it.

The reasons for calling the conference at Swanwick are now clear. It sprang from a sense of frustration with formal, time-wasting ecumenical schemes. Even the 'professional' ecumenical activists were tired of the treadmill of meetings and dead ends. There was also a growing desire for the 'spirit' rather than the form. So it is that the preface to the Swanwick Declaration, when speaking of this 'spirit' at the conference, says that it was 'not so much an *achieved* agreement, as that unity of heart and mind in common commitment to each other in Christ was received as a *gift*'.

A glimpse of unity?

'Not Strangers but Pilgrims' (NSBP), as the conference was called, was the 'national focus of the whole process which began with Lent 86'.[203] The Lenten Bible Study courses had been a success among the different churches that had taken part, with the kind of cross-fertilization that had hardly been realized previously. Over 330 representative members of the Inter-Church Process and others were brought together in Derbyshire. Things were moving from when it could be said 'In the ordinary life of the churches and local parishes the ecumenical movement has only just begun ... local level lags far behind the bold and lofty thrusts of the world ecumenical conferences'.[204]

Swanwick was a historic, significant and even 'deeply spiritual' conference for the participants. 'Those who took part in this conference were, mostly, experienced men and women, not easily bowled over emotionally; minds, patterns of thought were changed, convictions formed, commitments entered into', said the BCC.[205] Those who attended testified to a deep sense of the presence of God and the Holy Spirit at work.

But because a basic biblical conviction worked out in a systematic theology governs the evangelical mind, it is not likely that a conference could change patterns of thought. And the over-optimism of the conference spilled over in inaccuracies and impossibilities in its published documents. Some who signed the closing document were not even representatives of their churches and others, such as those from the Brethren churches, were probably at the conference without their sister assemblies' knowledge at all. And no-one could sign on behalf of a multitude of independent congregations. Hence the statement makes an inauspicious start: 'Appointed by our churches and under the guidance of the Holy Spirit we declare that this, the broadest assembly of British and Irish churches ever to meet in these islands has reached a common mind.'

Nevertheless, there is a passionate sense of occasion and longing, a great advance from the vain seeking after structures of previous ecumenical initiatives: 'Driven on by a gospel imperative to seek unity that the world may believe, we rejoiced that we are pilgrims together and strangers no longer.' It is perhaps inevitable that there is a touch of 'ecumenese' about this, of which William Temple himself would have been proud, for it is difficult to envisage how else such documents could express consensus. But they recognized diversity within the body of Christ:

> Unity is a gift of God. With gratitude we have truly experienced this gift, growing amongst us in these days. We affirm our openness to this growing unity in obedience to the Word of God, so that we may fully share, hold in common and offer to the world those gifts which we have received and still hold in separation. In the unity we seek we recognize that there will not be uniformity but legitimate diversity.

The old antipathy

But the potential for evangelical antipathy was just below the surface, for under the heading 'Working Together' is the following statement: 'Competitive evangelism is no longer acceptable'. Without actually identifying the area of evangelism to which they refer, or who they imagine the competitors to be, these words crystallize the ecumenical debate at the evangelical's most sensitive point. Under the heading 'Mission and Service' the report says that we are to share the good news in word and deed and agrees 'that Christian faith is of its very nature missionary ... Mission embraces explicit evangelism – that proclamation of the gospel which seeks to evoke a personal response of commitment to Christ and his Church.' Yet it is not clear whether 'competitive' refers to evangelism being strident, or pro-active or amongst other churches in 'pilgrimage'. What remains clear, however, is that an evangelical is one who presents the gospel to anyone, from any background, denomination or culture, if there is an appropriate opportunity to do so. An evangelical is by nature evangelistic.

Despite its warm and spiritual tone, this document does not address the fundamental impetus for evangelism – that Jesus saves us from our sin:

> Outreach includes sharing the Gospel with those, in Britain and beyond, in urban and rural areas, who are powerless, oppressed and often alienated by the churches; with those, in Britain and beyond, who are complacent, rich and powerful and who must hear God's word of challenge to them spoken boldly; with those we encounter in daily life whose lives may be empty or who long for a more inspiring and sustaining meaning to their work and life, and who have yet to hear Christians giving reasons for the hope that is in them.

However legitimate this might sound, for an evangelical the gospel is not about longing that people might have 'a more inspiring and sustaining meaning to their work and life'. And so as the Ecumenical Movement finally addressed the very matter over which evangelicals had been concerned for so long, as it moved forward using a new vocabulary that the evangelical could understand, it became clear to some that time-honoured tenets of faith had been marginalized, and to others that the inherent sensitivities of the theologically conservative had been brought to light.

Another problem for the evangelical was the breadth of involvement in the new *Ecumenical Instruments* documents.

The *Aims and Principles* are not contentious in themselves save in their assumptions. Yet the titles 'Not Strangers but Pilgrims' and 'Churches Together' raised some painful questions for evangelicals. Were they on the same pilgrimage as some of the disparate groups represented in the document?

All the old fears, questions and even prejudices came flooding back. What is the true church? Where it is to be found? How it is to be recognized? Derek Tidball has described evangelicalism as 'a subculture with its own ethos'. And the perennial problem for evangelicals within the Ecumenical Movement is that 'The ties which bind [evangelicals] together, diverse though they are, are also the ties that bind them apart from other groups within the church.'[206] An evangelical understands words like 'church' and 'evangelism' in a certain prescribed way – not more so than many a Roman Catholic, Anglo-Catholic or Orthodox, but the premises are different. The evangelical emanates a confidence as to revealed truth and his or her place within it that, among those outside these parameters, often breeds despair and difficulties that goodwill finds difficult to surmount. The evangelical mind, with its absolutes and convictions, is always going to be the problem child of ecumenism.

For example, the Unitarian Church is listed among the participants and observers at Swanwick. This provoked a strong reaction from evangelicals. Evangelicals could not even begin to discuss evangelism with a church that denies the deity of Christ, let alone go on pilgrimage together. Churches Together eventually realized this incompatibility, although it seemed not to notice that its Trinitarian formula of faith precludes Unitarians. Though Unitarians evolved from the historic Dissenters, their creedal position, or lack thereof, means that they are further from evangelicals than Roman Catholics.

Although evangelical attitudes to Roman Catholics have changed, to be formally and closely aligned in a national ecumenical endeavour, with the inevitable practical considerations of joint services, pulpit exchanges and joint evangelism, was more than some evangelicals could countenance. Many evangelicals in the main-line denominations were happy to be loosely identified with these new ecumenical initiatives, but for others the implications of any involvement were too complex and the theological price too high.

So here is the conundrum. The movement that ecumenical historians identify as beginning amongst evangelicals grew into something from which they increasingly felt alienated. Although this is sad, there is something even sadder yet. The greatest disaster for evangelicals themselves, besides the continuing disunity of the church, is that along the way evangelicals have become separated from one another. Perhaps, then, the primary ecumenical search must begin amongst themselves. Unless action is taken soon, the gulf between different factions of evangelicalism will become unbridgeable. If this happens, never again will they be able to speak with one voice to the wider church – for which, according to their cherished distinctives, they have a responsibility.

16

Barriers Begin to Crumble

Despite the disenchantment that many evangelicals have felt with structured ecumenism, the movement has helped to engender a certain self-recognition amongst Christians of different groups which has grown up parallel to it. As we will see later, through this self-recognition evangelical separatists have come to understand themselves as a 'party' within evangelicalism. Their negativism towards all things ecumenical has deepened, and their distrust of those outside themselves has increased. We must ask, then, what brought about this change of perception amongst Christians from different traditions. And what effect did it have amongst evangelicals themselves?

Building relationships

I think that Vatican II has had something to do with it. In early 1965, a Roman Catholic barrister friend came to a service at my home church with the reluctant permission of his priest, on the condition that he did not shut his eyes during the prayers! Vatican II changed that. Significant advances in terms of Roman Catholic participation in the Ecumenical Movement came out of that council, and this was not purely negative in its effect on evangelical/ecumenical relations.

The conservative evangelical Hans Kung said that 'The fact that the reunion of separated Christians – ecumenism, to give it its inelegant and easily misunderstood Latin name – was discussed at the Second Vatican council at all was in itself an event in church history of incalculable consequence.'[207] For Roman Catholics it was significant both in terms of increased biblical interest and for contact with other Christians, including evangelicals and charismatics.

In what way do I consider the Roman Catholics' increased appetite for and participation in ecumenical activity significant for evangelicals? Let me give two examples, both of which may be controversial depending on where a person stands on these issues. When I was a minister in Richmond, West London, I became friendly with the local Roman Catholic priest whom I met from time to time at local church events and at what were then described in non-PC terms as 'fraternals'. He asked me to preach in his church. When I demurred he said, 'Listen, Robert, you can preach on anything you like – there is no proviso because I trust you.' While some might consider this a wonderful gospel opportunity, I declined – not because preaching at his church would have been a compromise, but because it was a matter of common courtesy as it was impossible for me to return the invitation.

The other story is that a few years ago I was leading a holiday Bible week in Kilkee, County Clare, Ireland. There is but one lovely Church of Ireland minister for the whole county. He asked me if I would be prepared to make a broadcast on the local Roman Catholic radio station. I readily agreed. The priest responsible for the programme came to the hotel with his tape recorder. Within the administrative Catholic structures of the diocese his opportunity for more spiritual ministry was this radio station. As it transpired, he asked me to make two programmes. One was a devotional talk on the Bible passage for the week and the other was on how to conduct personal Bible study. I was thrilled. What is more, many Roman Catholic people – nuns and lay people – were regular and appreciative attendees at the evening Bible readings.

Both of these encounters resulted from Vatican II. Roman Catholics, particularly in Ireland, are in regular contact with evangelicals and vice versa. And I am not alone in being thankful to God for the stand that the Roman Catholic Church takes in moral and ethical matters today when many of our own churches seem crippled by dumbness. There is a firmness about the Roman Catholic's ecumenical relationships that the evangelical's approach should mirror – a mixture of courtesy and inflexible resolve.

My two stories will perhaps annoy people from all areas of the theological spectrum. The impression is that evangelicals – at least of my ilk – will take opportunities to exercise ministry but will not receive ministry in return. This is not true, and even at a subconscious level there is a cross-fertilization taking place across all denominations that is difficult to codify. Whether this is a negative or positive development depends, again, on one's perspective.

Theology

Over the past decades there has been, generally speaking, a move away from the radical liberalism that marked ecumenical activity and conversations in the inter-war years. Karl Barth (e.g., his commentary on Romans) and Emil Brunner brought a new biblical emphasis to broader theological thought. While this shift did not affect evangelicals, wider sections of the church began to take this scholarship on board with the result that evangelicals discovered they could converse more easily than they could previously.

The 1950s and 1960s marked the nadir of regard (or disregard, as the case may be) for evangelical biblical scholarship. InterVarsity Fellowship and other groups sought to rectify this. Yet the 'Honest to God' debate of the early 1960s and the 'death of God' ideas mooted in the late 1960s and early 1970s hardly seem to indicate the 'end of the Modernistic Movement'. What is clearer is that the theological atmosphere became somewhat more accommodating during this time. Evangelicals began to hold more significant positions throughout the ecclesiastical world – from bishops in the Church of England to men like F.F. Bruce in the academic world. None of this could have happened if evangelicals had kept themselves separate from the rest of the church. People will only listen to and assimilate evangelical scholarship through this kind of interaction.

Worship style and liturgy

Some of the fears and suspicions of previous generations with regard to the worship styles and liturgy of churches from other traditions began to dissipate as well. This was not so much a theological shift as a pragmatic recognition that some phobias were more cultural than creedal, shibboleths that had more to do with the traditions of the elders than with what the Bible says.

As a boy, I remember attending an Anglican church in Bristol for a Keswick relay.[208] Seeing others kneel to pray, I did likewise. My mother tapped me on the shoulder and said, 'We don't do that, we're Baptists!' But now, having emerged from some of the entrenched positions of the past, we feel more at home with each other.

The Baptists, a significant proportion of whom, as we have seen, have always been evangelical, experienced a liturgical movement which resulted in a cross-fertilization of prayers and lectionaries. The result was that they began to recognize features of each other's services and to feel more at ease with different forms than they had previously. A broad range of publications dealing with 'spirituality' and prayer from different generations and traditions followed.

In the 1960s, spiritual classics such as *The Imitation of Christ* by Thomas à Kempis and *A Serious Call to a Devout and Holy Life* by William Law were reprinted and widely read. Exposure to these ideas, though not perhaps perceived at the time, did influence evangelicals and their consideration of Christians outside of their usual areas of contact. Today evangelicals are exploring everything from the songs emanating from the Charismatic Movement, Celtic spirituality and prayers, liturgies and songs from Taizé and Graham Kendrick, to the wonderful hymns coming from New Frontiers International.

Laity

Another indication of crumbling barriers, though it is hard to quantify, is the changing function and role of the laity. Evangelicals have always been suspicious of 'priest-craft' and 'clergy-craft' of any description, but Till argues that the old battle cry of 'the priesthood of all believers' became 'more widely understood' than it once was.[209] While this might sound like music to evangelical ears, its only effect was incidental. There is little evidence of any breakdown of the 'priestly' role in some areas. But the individual church member is thinking differently and independently. On more than one occasion I have met people I know at events like Spring Harvest who have said, 'Don't tell my minister I'm here!' Church members have become an unruly lot outside of their own constituencies, and this has helped to break down barriers.

This change has little if anything to do with the Ecumenical Movement. Many Christians in England were moving away from old entrenched positions in a number of areas, and in doing so were beginning to recognize each other as brothers and sisters in Christ. This shift reached evangelicals in the main-line denominations, if not those in the more separatist traditions.

One barrier crumbles, another appears ...

For many evangelicals, the fears and prejudices – and, some would think, the convictions – of the past were beginning to dissipate. As people met, for example, during weeks of prayer for Christian unity, as Roman Catholics and evangelicals stood together on some of the social issues such as abortion and euthanasia, as local councils of churches met together and various evangelistic missions brought wide-ranging support and contact across denominational and theological boundaries, there grew a mutual recognition of each other as people of faith. These natural outworkings of trust achieved more than the great ecumenical conferences, with their erudite, theologically rounded pronouncements, could ever have done. Christians of all persuasions, outside the rarefied ecumenical debating chambers, began to live out their personal and corporate faith.

Although evangelicals had little interest in ecumenical structures, they were drawn to the movement because it brought Christians together. It was a two-way process. After having been ignored for so long, the evangelical voice was beginning to be heard, and the fears of some evangelicals were a little assuaged. But how this degree of confidence was built across a wide spectrum of evangelical thought is a complex matter. For the very matters that have been an encouragement to some have been serious concerns for others. Building a sense of unity in one part of the evangelical constituency has meant alienating another. And it is that divide that is my chief concern.

17

Roman Catholic Involvement

Churches Together in England included Roman Catholics. In any previous generation, official Roman Catholic participation in the ecumenical process would have meant the withdrawal of certain denominations, such as the Baptists. Yet this fundamental change in perceptions and attitudes which we have been exploring meant that, by 1987, Roman Catholic involvement was far more accepted by many across the evangelical spectrum. Whether this is a development to be lauded or criticized depends on one's perspective.

How could a denomination like the Baptists be part of an ecumenical enterprise with Roman Catholic involvement (unofficially in 1987 and officially in 1990)? The greatest ecumenical barrier for Baptists had, apparently, been surmounted – and it happened quickly, but at the cost of increasing evangelical disunity.

There was no appetite for fresh ecumenical initiatives amongst Christians – Roman Catholics included – and a more empathetic spirit grew among them. The inclusion of Roman Catholics has a fundamental bearing on evangelical ecumenical attitudes. The question features constantly in the debate among evangelicals, and so we need to understand the issues before we can hope to build evangelical unity. In addition, main-line evangelical thinking on the topic has changed over the last twenty years, and it is important to understand the reasons for this.

As recently as 1978, Michael Ramsey, then Archbishop of Canterbury, commented with some ecumenical optimism that the 'progress within the ecumenical movement had been miraculous' and 'only a few more divine miracles – and they do happen – will bring us all to that day of unity in truth and holiness, total unity in the Mass given to us by Jesus'.[210] Certainly Ramsey was not being sensitive to evangelicals (nor was he probably even thinking of them) when he used the admittedly innocuous but emotive word 'Mass'. Perhaps no other single word could be so effective in raising theological sensitivities and phobias in the minds and hearts of a whole section of a Christian community. While within a decade of Ramsey's statement the ecumenical 'movement' had come to a virtual standstill, a change had taken place in attitudes between Christians that might indeed be described as 'miraculous'.

When entering into 'Churches Together', the strong residual grass-roots concern over inter-church involvement with Roman Catholics was either forgotten or ignored by some leaders. Old fears and present theological convictions could not be dealt with at a stroke – nor perhaps should they be. Even J.H. Shakespeare, head of the BU a century previously, would have been shocked by Ramsey's statement. He was hardly thinking of the Mass when he said, 'A great change has passed over men's minds in relation to Christian unity.' Shakespeare was firm in his belief that a united church should be 'based on the evangelical faith and on the principles of the Reformation'. Contrast this with the Swanwick Declaration (the precursor to 'Churches Together'), where the signatories declared a 'clear commitment to each other ... in common evangelism'. This was a 'new beginning' such as Shakespeare could hardly have even dreamt of – for an understanding of the nature of the gospel, which must be the precursor to joint evangelism, had not even been addressed. Some evangelical concern, therefore, was inevitable.

Archbishop Temple's ecumenical credentials were faultless, yet apparently he did not have unity with the Roman Catholic Church much more in mind than had Shakespeare before him. He said, 'Some day, no doubt, in a very remote future, the question of union with Rome will become practical. At present I regard it as almost infinitely remote'. In large measure Ramsey was right, and apparently Temple's expectation was too limited. The attitudes of many evangelicals towards Roman Catholics, if not towards the Roman Catholic Church as an institution, have perceptibly altered over the last thirty years.

The Roman Catholic historian Hastings wrote of this period between the mid-1980s and mid-1990s: 'A sense of one Christian community with a common mission and a common faith had become central to the experience of all main churches in England in a way that it had never been previously. And that was a very great achievement.'[211] This 'great achievement' is not the uniting of denominational structures, which all agreed had failed. Temple's scepticism regarding organic union had been confirmed by the Anglican decision in 1993 to ordain women. This step put thought of union between Anglicanism and Rome back another generation at least. But it was perceptions, if not structures, that were changing.

While no evangelical has taken on board any of the Catholic doctrines, or anything like it, their change of attitude is witnessed, for example, by their being part of the Anglican Roman Catholic International Commission (ARCIC) and signing the 'Swanwick Declaration' and joining 'Churches Together'. The participants and observers at Swanwick included various Baptist Unions, the West Indian Evangelical Alliance, Christian Brethren and others, all of whom would have a majority of evangelical adherents. The attitude of Roman Catholics had changed, too, for after many years of being officially apart from the Ecumenical Movement they were also signatories at Swanwick. This shift was partly, as we have seen, a result of Vatican II. As Hastings noted, 'the Vatican Council then set in motion a vast process which, with qualifications, can, not unreasonably, be seen as the Protestantization of the modern Catholic Church'. While the extent to which this judgment is correct is debatable, many, including evangelicals, shared this perception.

Evangelicals perceived a new openness among Roman Catholics, in the 'first world' at least, to the Bible. They also noted and approved the publication of the widely used and respected 'Jerusalem Bible' as well as the unequivocal stance that Roman Catholics were taking on moral issues of particular concern to evangelicals such as abortion and euthanasia. There also grew a certain respect among evangelicals for the Roman Catholic 'conservative' stand on certain fundamental doctrines. Roman Catholics did not seem to be quite the threat previously either imagined or portrayed.

Separatists had largely avoided involvement with Billy Graham's missions in England. Because of the Anglican David Watson's embracing attitude towards Roman Catholics, separatists avoided his missions in the 1970s and mid-1980s. Yet the Charismatic Movement, with which many main-line evangelicals were involved, removed many boundaries amongst main-line evangelicals. Protestant and Catholic charismatics met and worshipped together, sang the same songs, read the same books and began to recognize each other as Christians of similar experience. The rapidly spreading and flexible Charismatic Movement connected Christians from different traditions and backgrounds.

William Oddie, a convert to the Roman Catholic Church from the Anglican ministry who is now a journalist, described this growing empathy between evangelicals and Roman Catholics. 'The Reformation, after all, was supposed to be all about the authority of Holy Scripture: but these days, if you take the Bible seriously, you will have to become either a conservative evangelical or a Roman Catholic.'[212]

Though overtly evangelical, events such as Spring Harvest, which started in the late 1970s, increased contacts across the Protestant divide and laid low historic 'bogeymen'. Separatists, however, generally saw this kind of interaction as dangerous: 'The combination of mass evangelism and the excitement of the charismatic renewal had become caught up with and harnessed by the Ecumenical Movement', said one sceptical commentator.[213]

The 1966 National Assembly of Evangelicals first highlighted this division between separatists and other evangelicals, and from that moment the two groups increasingly went their own ways. No longer could the noun 'evangelical' describe one group of people in the wider church. Evangelical was used more frequently as an adjective, describing a disparate group of parties within and without the main-line denominations. Though many fundamental truths still linked them, different emphases, parties, suspicions and even rancour divided evangelicals. Ecumenical trends as we have seen above, complicated by the Charismatic Movement, only intensified the distance. These groups established their own leaders, spokespeople and publications. Although EA and the BEC (later to be called Affinity) made some effort to bridge the gap, in truth it was widening – and widening fast.

The EA, particularly in the later 1980s as it experienced rapid growth, made its main appeal to evangelicals in the denominations and the new charismatic groupings.

Membership in the EA was regarded as almost the benchmark of orthodoxy – not only among churches and individuals, but also among the mushrooming 'industry' of evangelical para-church organizations.

The BEC was founded in 1953 and grew not so much in numbers as it did in influence as the focal point and mouthpiece for separatism – especially as polarization amongst evangelicals increased. The *Evangelical Times*, founded in 1967 (and latterly the more embracing *Evangelicals Now*, founded in 1986) enabled non-charismatic 'principled separatism' to have a voice, said David Bebbington.[214] The separatists were becoming increasingly articulate as they formulated their opposition to ecumenism. If they were becoming more intransigent, the same could not be said of evangelicals in the main-line denominations, and in Anglicanism in particular.

It was perhaps in the Church of England and through John Stott, one of its leaders, that the most dramatic change was to be seen in main-line evangelical ecumenical attitudes. In 1967, the first Anglican Evangelical Congress was held at Keele. It demonstrated that evangelicals at that time were a marginalized group within the Anglican Church. By the second congress, held in April 1977, things had changed, due in no small part Stott's influence. Because Stott is generally regarded as the leader of this group of main-line evangelicals even to this day, it will be helpful to study his ecumenical contribution in some depth.

John Stott

At the Church Leaders' Conference held in Birmingham in 1972, when over five hundred leaders including the Archbishop of Canterbury and Cardinal Heenan were present, John Stott was part of the commission on 'Evangelism'. For Stott this was a risky venture, for he was in far from conservative evangelical company. 'He spoke with Michael Taylor, the Principal of the Northern Baptist College who had been in trouble with his fellow-Baptists for an alleged Christological heresy.' This was not Stott's usual constituency. 'Sentence by sentence, John Stott worked through John 17 with the challenging assumption that it stated the wishes of Jesus himself for the ecumenical movement.'[215] Quite clearly Stott was consciously walking a path that very few conservative evangelicals before him had walked.

At the Lausanne Conference on World Evangelism in July 1974, Billy Graham took a clear anti-ecumenical stand: 'This must be a gathering of those committed to the evangelical position as we understand it. This should not be a gathering of those committed to liberal or to controversial positions'. The American Arthur Johnston said, 'The planning of Lausanne, isolated the heretical views of the ecumenical movement, exposed their non-biblical foundations and strongly reaffirmed the primacy of proclamation evangelism.'[216] At that time, it would seem, the traditional evangelical attitudes to Christians of other traditions still prevailed.

Yet John Stott, who was Lausanne's principal theoretician, author of its introductory study, *The Biblical Basis of Evangelism*, and chairman of the follow-up committee, the Lausanne Theological and Education Group, seemed to be quietly steering Lausanne in the very directions which Johnston was denouncing. It was due to Stott, according to Hastings, that the Lausanne Covenant avoided a commitment to the verbal inspiration of Scripture; made social action a partner of evangelicalism; and stressed, instead of individual and undenominational evangelism, the collective responsibility of the visible church. None of this was acceptable to American evangelicals. In the words of one commentator, 'Stott seemed to be leading the movement back on to the slippery slope which was believed to have been so fatal half a century before in the days of the SCM, so disastrous to the WCC, the very road which had led to the undermining of all the simple certainties of the early missionary movement.'[217]

In December 1976, speaking at a conference of African evangelicals in Nairobi, John Stott admitted that he had been present as an adviser at the WCC conference in Nairobi the year before. 'It seems to me that evangelicals ought to be in the World Council', he said.[218] Stott was treading on dangerous ground as far as many evangelicals were concerned.

By the second Anglican Evangelical Congress at Nottingham in 1977, the shift towards a more embracing stance towards other churches and in such areas as social involvement, was clear. Stott chaired this congress as he had the first, ten years earlier. 'Evangelicals ought to be conservative on the bible and radical on everything else', he said. Mainstream evangelical Anglicans had become radical, particularly in regard to the Ecumenical Movement. Of Stott, Hastings observed,

> The accepted patriarch of English Evangelicalism, he had moved steadily forward in his own thinking, and had struggled with skill and determination to liberate evangelicalism from its narrowness and overcome the schisms within Protestant Christianity between ecumenicals and Evangelicals, which had dogged it since almost the start of the century. Indeed on almost all the issues where Evangelicals had been accustomed to point the finger at the former, Stott had come down in defence of the wider ecumenical position, always carefully phrased but increasingly unequivocal. Within the world Evangelical movement of the second half of the century he played to Billy Graham a role not altogether unlike that which J.H. Oldham had played fifty years before to John R. Mott. In each case the

less flamboyant but more intellectual Englishman was
endeavouring to guide the movement into new, less simplistic vistas.[219]

It is doubtful whether Stott was undertaking a conscious
effort to redirect evangelicalism. And yet this quotation is
not without considerable significance. Although much of
the above has not been widely quoted in evangelical circles,
the regard in which Stott is still rightly held, and the fact
that IVP still publishes his commentaries and other writings, indicate a tolerance amongst mainstream evangelicals
that would not have been present but a generation previously. Stott had captured a mood among many evangelicals
in the main-line denominations and more tolerant separatists, and charted a course that was highlighted in the
confrontation between him and Martyn Lloyd-Jones in
1966, as we have seen.

This change of attitude among evangelicals of which we
have been speaking did not reveal itself so much in overt
activity within ecumenism, which was still rare other than
for denominational leaders, but rather in a preparedness
either to let sleeping dogs lie, or to live, if uneasily, with the
status quo. Whereas previously only denominational leaders participated in the never-ending ecumenical conference
scene, now amongst many evangelicals in a denomination
like the Baptists, for instance, there was either a resigned
acquiescence to the new ecumenical structures or a comparatively muted protest.

The EA, of which so many evangelicals were members,
reflected this change of emphasis in the wider arena to a
degree, yet it did so studiously apart from any overt ecumenical identification. There were contacts between the EA
and ecumenical leaders of some significance, but these
were not made public, and their importance must not be
overstated. I was a participant in ad hoc meetings that were

regularly held in the early 1990s between the officers of the EA and BCC – meetings which were neither publicized nor minuted.

There have been careless statements from those who wish to overstate this shift, such as 'old-fashioned Protestants have died out'.[220] This is hardly true, for there are still organizations with strongly Protestant sympathies operating in the Anglican context. Even now, David Watson's careless remark that the Reformation was a tragedy is not given more credence by evangelicals than it was at the time.[221]

Amongst evangelicals in the non-denominational and separatist streams, the negative attitude to anything that smacked of ecumenism became ever more vociferous when the BEC began producing the *Ecumenical Digest*. The first edition in 1995 described its purpose: 'It consists of extracts from various publications which illustrate contemporary ecumenism. These indicate today's regrettable trend away from biblical principles.' Separatist fear of, and antagonism towards, the 'compromised' evangelicals within the mainline denominations were startlingly confirmed in unexpected ways.

18

Theological Problems Posed by the Unity Debate

While it was a fairly straightforward matter to establish the biblical mandate for unity, we have seen from history the multitude of theological and practical difficulties that pursuing unity presents. The last thing I wish to do here, as we flesh out some of these theological problems, is to dismiss or ridicule anyone. Christ's prayer for the church to be one makes the matter too important for point scoring. What follows is not an evolution from, or an addition to, evangelical doctrine. Nor is it a declension or an abrogation from evangelicalism, but rather a natural and consistent pragmatic demonstration of it – I hope!

When it began in 1947 the WCC, with contributions from some of the most eminent theologians of the day, laid down a clear theological foundation. *The Universal Church in God's Design* was published in 1948. In the introduction Van Dusen said, 'The Church carries a large share of responsibility for man's disorder; and it is for that responsibility that the churches must give account.' Or as he puts it more succinctly, 'The fundamental problem of the Church is the churches.' Evangelicals, as a part of the church, share something of that responsibility.[222]

Although there are many churches, the ideal New Testament church does not exist. 'It ought to be holy, but it is not. It ought to be universally one, but it is not,' said Julian Charley (later to become a leading Anglican ecumenist) in one of the papers given to the EA assembly in 1966.[223] But that does not mean we are to accept the status quo as normative. As we have seen from Scripture, the church is the bride and body of Christ, and evangelicals as much as any others have no option but to work, however difficult and uncomfortable that might be, for the unity of the church.

To accomplish this, all of us will have to give up the Romantic individualism in which we have gloried. While personal salvation is certainly a prerequisite to being a member of the church, evangelicals have stressed individualism in the past in a way that is unhelpful. While the church is the community of those with saving faith, it is more than that. Julian Charley, in the paper to the EA assembly in 1966 referred to above, suggests a move away from individualism. The church is the Lord's (Acts 2:47) and not subject to human definition. Charley describes as Pelagian the view of those who argue that where 'two or three are gathered' in the name of Christ, there is the church. This interpretation has, he says, 'produced a man-centred doctrine of the Church'. *Kyriakon* is the Lord's house, more than it is the people who meet in it. 'The Lord added to their number' for 'he knows those who are his' (1 Tim. 2:19). The responsibility for who is added to the church belongs with God.

As a Baptist, the doctrine of the 'gathered church' is a central one for me. But for those who hold the doctrine, the search for unity often seems to be pointless. If the church is constituted only of the 'faithful' who have been converted, then why endeavour to build bridges towards others who, because they do not seem to fulfil the evangelical criteria of membership, are not part of the 'true' church? The stumbling block to that position is that the Lord himself does not allow it. He prays that the church may be one, knowing full well that it is not.

The New Testament churches were very different from each other and the membership criteria are sketchy. Yet it is clear that where Jesus is declared as Lord (Phil. 2:11), there is the church. Not every church, obviously, is a member of the church universal. But no-one has the authority to say who is a member and who is not. Even evangelical churches, with all their checks and balances, can hardly imagine that their church consists only of the redeemed. (That is not, of course, to imply that evangelicals should be careless in their theological convictions or apply no criteria for membership.)

Peter Masters, in the booklet *Separation and Obedience*, effectively caricatures the argument:

> It is our duty to stay in denominations no matter how bad they become, and also to co-operate in our evangelism with those who do not share evangelical views, because the Lord tells us that His Church is bound to contain good and bad elements until the Day of Judgment. The parable of the wheat and tares tells us not to attempt to secure a pure Church, but to let both grow together until harvest.[224]

For Masters, the field of Matthew 13:24 'represents the world not the Church at all', and in that he might be right. But he has not invalidated the argument, for in the parable of the net that immediately follows, the net is not the world.

William Hendriksen says of the passage:

> However, not all of those that enter the kingdom in its visible manifestation – for all practical purposes we might as well say not all those who enter the church visible – are truly saved.

This will be evident in the great day of judgment when the angels will separate the wicked from the righteous.[225]

When Hendriksen argues that the separation is to be an eschatological one, he is in agreement with the *Baptist Confession of 1689*, to which Masters also would subscribe. It says, 'the purest churches under heaven are subject to mixture and error. Nevertheless Christ always will (to the end of time) have a kingdom in this world'.

It is important for every believer to be part of a church that is as doctrinally pure as possible and best expresses one's convictions. Nevertheless, a future eschatological separation carries with it the corollary that now is the time for the church to seek the unity for which Christ prayed. 'Now' is always the time in Scripture for dealing with our relationship with God and humankind.

G.K.A. Bell, former Bishop of Chichester and the foremost Anglican ecumenist after William Temple, also speaks of this eschatological dimension but believes it to be more immediate and therefore more pressing: 'The choice which has to be made is between Christ and the anti-Christ. It may be sooner than we know that those who are united on the side of Christ will be compelled to stand together visibly, in spite of denominational differences.'[226]

Lesslie Newbigin also refers to an eschatological dimension when he writes in *What Is the Local Church?* of the 'unity which will be fully manifest only when God has completed his purpose to sum up all things in Christ. The local church will be a credible sign of that eschatological unity when it is moving towards it.'[227] Sadly, some seem to be moving away from what will be an eschatological certainty of one united church.

For evangelicals, the authority of the church is self-contained. Structures, authorities such as bishops and 'marks' such as the sacraments, though not unimportant, are secondary. This has more to do with the doctrines that it holds than with its membership: 'We judge a church by its professed standards of faith, and not by the opinions of individuals within it,' said Frank Colquhoun.[228]

The best starting place for building unity, then, is for local churches to speak together – such communication is a primary way for building up evangelical confidence. The church 'is the local expression of the family of God, that is the community focus in spirituality', said David Gillett.[229] While this is true, the church is much more than that. Evangelical aspirations for unity often end when a single truth is overemphasized.

While we 'guard against a rigid spirit which denies the essential liberty of the gospel', as Colquhoun says, there are limits as well. The New Testament instructs us here as well. When some cardinal doctrine came into question among the early churches, the councils addressed it immediately and with conviction. For, as Paul says, another 'gospel' is no gospel at all (Gal. 1:7). The gospel leaves no room for equivocation concerning its fundamental truths, but neither does it allow any of us to consider ourselves the sole possessors of its truth. When Jesus asked that the Father might 'sanctify them by the truth' (Jn. 17:17) there was no either/or between unity and the truth, nor one at the cost of the other. The dangers then, as today, lie in a person or group either imagining that they alone have all truth or being negligent with the truth. As we have seen in this chapter, the first option is not open to us. The second is called syncretism, and we turn to examine that now.

The danger of syncretism

A syncretistic church has nothing to offer the world and no distinctive message with which to gain its attention. There are those who have argued that the modern ecumenical movement has led, in some cases, to syncretism. Alan Morrison has characterized the movement of ecumenism as 'A universal brotherhood of Christian faith leading to a universal brotherhood of religious faith which in turn leads to a universal brotherhood of mankind.'[230] In his second BBC Reith Lecture in 1978, Dr Edward Norman, then Dean of Peterhouse, Cambridge, rightly noted that 'The word ecumenical itself has changed its meaning, and is now used by the WCC to mean, not just fellowship within the different Christian bodies, but within the entire human race.'[231] Morrison quotes Dr Ursula King, lecturer in theology at Leeds University and founder of the Teilhard de Chardin Centre: 'We are in need of a global, worldwide ecumenism which goes beyond the ecumenism of the Christian churches by being truly universal.'[232] Although many Christians who work within the auspices of the WCC and other ecumenical organizations would deny such a statement, there must be concern when a WCC report says:

> It was assuming that the purpose of mission was Christianization, bringing man to God through Christ and his church. Today the fundamental question is much more that of true Man, and the dominant concern of the missionary congregation must therefore be to point to the humanity in Christ as the goal of mission.[233]

The commission of the church, however, is to preach the gospel (Mt. 28:19).

Visser't Hooft himself was fearful of this possibility in the WCC, and he wrote that syncretism was 'a far more dangerous challenge to the Christian church than fully-fledged atheism is ever likely to be'. The gospel, he said, 'is to be given in its purest form ... in accordance with the biblical witness and unmixed with extraneous or cultural elements'.[234]

John Stott was reported as saying at the 1975 Nairobi Assembly of the WCC, 'in listening to the cry of the oppressed they were also listening to the cry of the lost. If justice means the upholding of people's rights, is not one of the most fundamental rights the right to hear the gospel?'[235] At that same assembly in Nairobi a few, including the then Bishop of London Graham Leonard, walked out in protest over their impotence to change the syncretistic direction of the WCC. Whether Stott's or Leonard's was the more significant contribution, Stott rightly recognized that the Ecumenical Movement needs to hear what evangelicals have to say about mission, and they have taken opportunities to do so. Unless the gospel is central, syncretism is inevitable. As leaders, Stott and Leonard take their responsibility and authority seriously. One remains in the process and the other walks out – this image encapsulates the debate that this book endeavours to present.

19

Where Does Authority Lie?

Christians concede delegated authority to ministers and other leaders and are to obey and pray for them so that their work will be a joy (Heb. 13:17). We have discussed the authority of Scripture, but we also need to examine the biblical basis for authority figures in the church. Many evangelicals react negatively, and often rightly so, to the 'princes of the church', whether papal or clerical. But saying that Scripture alone is sufficient is hardly satisfactory if there are many conflicting interpretations and understandings of Scripture. Where, then, does human authority lie?

Certainly the presbyter/bishop described in the New Testament has authority, but it is a different role to that often understood today. While the Old Testament describes Saul as a king/shepherd (2 Sam. 5:2), the New Testament picture is rather of a shepherd pastor – who is not like secular leaders, who lord it over their people (Mk. 10:42–45). However exalted a leader's name or position, their pronouncements are subject to Scripture. Godly leaders can lead but not push their people, and they cannot hold them back when these same people sense God's leading. So what, then, is the problem?

First, there has been a subtle shift. Evangelical identity and leadership have undergone considerable changes in recent years. According to ECONI (Evangelical

Contribution on Northern Ireland), a significant evangelical 'think tank', 'Evangelicals now define themselves in relation to other Evangelicals instead of to non-Evangelicals.' ECONI calls this 'Confessionalism', describing those who seek to justify their position within the evangelical constituency rather than relating to other sections of the church. So it could be said that 'this kind of evangelicalism found its unity in commonly owned, commonly confessed *truth*'.

This 'Confessionalism' describes many of us, but there are problems here. The paper argues that with the rise of evangelical confidence after the 1970s there grew 'Transconfessionalism', which is 'A shift from confessional substance to simple, organizational fraternity.' And the danger of this is that,

> the ground of relatedness among evangelicals ... has far less to do with living within the definitional parameters of what it meant to be evangelical and far more with belonging somewhere within the entrepreneurial and organizational life of this righteous empire.

And if that sounds academic and irrelevant to you, then think again. The consequences of this are important for evangelical unity and many other issues besides. Many evangelicals are nervous of being outside of their organized life of 'righteous empire'.

And in this light we can understand the comments of those I mentioned above who, at places like Spring Harvest or inter-church events say, 'Don't tell my minister I'm here!' Moving outside the group has not made them uncomfortable, but the authority of the group leader has. Obviously any self-respecting pastor or under-shepherd desires the best grass for his sheep and is anxious to keep them from the wolves. But sheep have minds of their own and, as we have seen, the biblical leader leads rather than drives. Any good pastor seeks to direct his flock to the best and safest food that is available. Although some sheep may wander off to new pastures they will, in my experience, return in time to the food that satisfies. But meanwhile there is not much that can be done, for at the lowest denominator local churches are voluntary organizations – and perhaps it is better that way.

In David Priors' commentary on 2 Corinthians he writes the following on Paul's words 'not that we lord it over your faith, but we work with you for your joy, because it is by faith you stand firm (2 Cor. 1:24):

> Paul is determined not to dominate or manipulate. The word used for 'lording it' is the verb from the Greek noun for 'Lord' as applied uniquely and incontrovertibly to Jesus in the New Testament – I believe over 400 times. It was the Greek form of '*imperator*', the Latin title for the Roman Emperor. Even more significantly it is the Greek word used in the Septuagint (the Greek translation of the Old Testament) for Yahweh, the name of God as revealed to Moses at his commissioning. Paul is unambiguously telling the Corinthians: 'Jesus is Lord, your Lord, and I will do nothing to usurp his pre-eminent place in your lives.' That is a searching truth for any person entrusted with pastoral responsibility, because it is all too easy to take the place of Jesus in someone's affections or allegiance.[237]

Over the years several people have come to our church from groups or churches that were very loving and supportive but also strongly directive, authoritarian, possessive and insular. And they were not Jehovah's Witnesses or Exclusive Brethren, but members of evangelical churches or umbrella organizations that used words like 'shepherding'. The danger is that these groups might have taken the place of Jesus in 'lording it over the faith' of their members. Christian maturity does not come that way.

Authority figures can make us feel safe and comfortable. Being given direction in all areas of faith and conduct can provide security. Yet, appealing though it may be, the authority that dominates is suspect, for 'if the Son shall make you free you will indeed be free'. Christians concede delegated authority to ministers and other leaders and are to obey and pray for them so that their work will be a joy.

But these authority figures disagree. While many use their God-given authority appropriately, some are involved in 'heavy shepherding' or the over-regulation of the life and conduct of their congregations. Others imply that they alone teach truth and provide fellowship. What those who wield authority in this way have in common is an insistence that to move beyond them or their fraternity is to move into acute danger. Church unity is only to be found amongst them.

So how do we handle the discrepancies between those who agree on the authority of Scripture yet still cannot agree sufficiently to build towards a structured unity? And what is to be done about those who seem unable to demonstrate their fellowship in the gospel with any other than themselves or others who hold to some similar minutia of secondary doctrine? This is where the analysis of modern evangelicalism given by ECONI and Carson becomes relevant. John Stott grapples with this problem in *The Contemporary Christian* when he speaks of the *adiaphora*, the 'matters indifferent', where liberty must be given. Till, too, is right when he says,

> The matter of authority is the critical debate for the ecumenical movement. For the divisions of the church and the search for its unity, turn fundamentally on the question of authority – the authority of the church, and authority in the

church. If this question could be solved, or some reasonable consensus reached, all others would fall into line.[238]

It would be simplistic and disingenuous of evangelicals, therefore, to imply that accepting Scripture as the sole authority is the only issue. In any group, tradition, the power of the minister and the constraints of the peer group are also considerations. While evangelicals accept and trumpet the sole authority of Scripture, inevitably there are many other authorities too. Nevertheless, Scripture is the place where matters of authority will be settled.

Unity amongst evangelicals and the wider church does not hang on a nuance of interpretation, solving a debate on authority, or settling some theological conundrum. Rather, the matter rests in the hands of ordinary church members and their instinctive sense of unease, believing that the church should be other than it is.

Lesslie Newbigin appreciated this importance of the people themselves when helping to form the Church of South India. Of the vociferous critics of the Union he wrote:

> They were thinking of a theological abstraction, not of living people; or – if any living people were in view – it was the denizens of the Methodist Chapel opposite the Parish Church, and not the villagers in far away India … I felt that it was perhaps more important to try simply to introduce the combatants to the living human being about whose spiritual interests they were supposed to be fighting.[239]

And so in the next chapter we will examine how bridges can be built between evangelicals themselves – between those whose confidence, trust and relationships have been fractured by ecumenical pressures. Then, and only then, will evangelicals be able to make constructive contributions to the wider search for unity.

20

Hindrances to Evangelical Unity

Some evangelicals refuse to interact with anyone, including other evangelicals. If they have the whole truth themselves, and know that others do not accept this truth, interaction is pointless. While other evangelicals rightly insist that differences do matter and need to be faced, they point out the differences but rarely address them. There is, therefore, no progress towards unity. It would be a denial of evangelical convictions to ignore the differences and an equal denial to refuse to address them in terms of mutual humility and respect.

None of this should be a threat to the cerebral evangelical mind that finds intellectual stability in the verities of the faith. Alan Gibson rebuts the accusation made of separatists 'that to call something *cerebral* is a put-down'. Yet for those who have thought through their doctrine, who are grounded in the faith, no movement – ecumenical or otherwise – should be frightening or cause vulnerability. John Shearer described the Swanwick Declaration as follows: 'The statement is so vague that it amounts to saying, in effect, "We agree to hold hands together in the dark, not knowing either who we are, where we are going, or where we will end up!"' Christ's command, by contrast, is to seek to bring some light to the situation.

It is this sense of the unknown that some evangelicals cannot accommodate in others or themselves. Yet being willing to be vulnerable may be one of the costs that evangelicals will need to pay to be part of a process that needs the light of truth they have to bring to the darkness. This is not new, for as Derek Tidball argues, 'Evangelicalism has never been the fixed and immutable entity that some would suggest.' To be truly cerebral is to grapple with intellectual issues rather than withdrawing when a contrary view is proposed.

Once the possibility of theological sharing is conceded, there is a further step to be taken. Evangelicals will only participate in wider debate if they see that unity is important. John Lawrence says that if 'the expressed objections of Conservative evangelicals were overcome ... visible unity might be desirable yet rank low in the order of priorities'.[241] Christ's prayer for the church would seem to dictate that a positive ecumenical contribution by evangelicals is essential. Unity is 'so that the world may believe' (Jn. 17:21) and is not a regression from cherished theological absolutes.

But refusing to take part in these conversations is easier in the short run than addressing divergent theological opinions. There is a consistency to the argument of the BEC that said in its 1986 council, 'there is need for separation from error in the world, false teaching in the Church and those supporting either. This would include for us separation from that form of ecumenicity which embraces those who deny Gospel essentials.'[242] This position offers the two attributes of logic and safety. But it is not a position the evangelical can hold consistently. If evangelicals are indeed bearers of 'good news', then they have something important to tell world. Speaking to the church means conversation in places where the church is listening for the contribution that evangelicals have to make in a spirit of good will. To the rejoinder of ACUTE (Evangelical Alliance Commission on Unity and Truth among Evangelicals) that 'Truth has always been more important than friendship',[243]

the evangelical would agree – for nothing short of the truth
will do. Yet standing for truth need not, indeed dare not, be
at the cost of interaction.

All of this is only an extension of what evangelicals have
always been prepared to do. As we have seen, evangelicals
can be willing to accommodate others on matters of the
greatest importance – such as baptism, episcopacy and
church government. As the Ecumenical Movement has discovered, in some sections of the church such matters are
cardinal truths and any form of accommodation is impossible. In the Calvinistic/Arminian debate neither position,
for example, though fundamentally different, would deny
the other the epithet of evangelical. Evangelicals have also
learned to co-exist despite differences in eschatology. No
one would expect evangelicals to sacrifice their convictions
any more than other sections of the church have sacrificed
theirs, but evangelicals can bring the accommodation they
have displayed amongst themselves into the wider church
both as an example and a precedent in the search for unity

There are matters of conviction over which the evangeli
cal must seem frustratingly intransigent to a non-evangeli
cal. ACUTE's *What Is an Evangelical?* lists no fewer than ten
doctrines 'which are non-negotiable', including the person
and work of Christ and the authority of Scripture
Evangelicals have to explain why they are prepared to
accommodate in certain areas that others see as essential
but yet not at all in the defence of the 'gospel' as they
believe it to be taught in Holy Scripture. The key word here
is explanation – not accommodation. For explanation to be
effective there must be those prepared to speak and listen
Accommodation is not the route towards unity among
evangelicals and beyond. If it were, the journey would have
been an easy walk and a 'world church' would already b
in place. Yet ecumenical history reveals that at Lima 198.
the WCC was willing and brave enough to grapple with

fundamental issues, without compromise. The report *Baptism, Eucharist and Ministry* may have solved nothing, but at least it grappled with major issues. Today, evangelicals and others have to be brave and strong enough to wrestle with similar issues – without compromise.

But it takes two parties to talk, and so it will never happen if evangelicals refuse to participate – and misunderstandings and caricatures of the positions of others will only continue to grow. To highlight the problems and then walk away and refuse to address them reveals a lack of integrity. But can such conversation lead to fruitful advance towards unity? As a necessary and consistent outworking of their convictions as evangelicals, as we have argued above, in time this interaction will bear fruit. God will bless their efforts, even if the road is long and hard and individuals don't actually see the fruit themselves. The responsibility to address the fundamental issues – as they are rather than as they are imagined to be – rests with the whole church.

While some eminent conservative evangelicals have refused to engage in theological conversations with Roman Catholics, evangelicals are leading the way in North America and Ireland by holding such discussions with Roman Catholics. The published document coming out of these conversations is called *Evangelicals and Catholics Together: The Christian Mission in the Third Millennium* (ETC, 1996). James Packer, Os Guinness and John White, amongst others, identified with this initiative in America. These are conservative evangelicals who would never concede any point of fundamental truth. But they were fulfilling their mandate as evangelicals.

When Packer says, 'Any contact he has had with the Catholics has been in the context of evangelical theology',[244] both he and the Roman Catholics are to be applauded, for contact and theology are at the heart of the search for unity.

The December 1994 edition of *Evangelicals Now* reported these discussions and, not surprisingly, various publications launched attacks against the evangelical participants. In reply, Packer says that the original statement was a

> co-belligerence document urging that Evangelicals and Catholics got together in making Christ known and standing for righteousness in the community, up to the limit of what they actually hold in common, i.e. the Apostles' Creed, plus the infallibility of Scripture, plus the nature of the Christian life as sustained by conversion to Christ.[245]

It is grounds for optimism when each side holds clearly expressed convictions graciously, yet firmly. It is only when the fundamentals are deflected, diluted or conveniently forgotten that evangelicals, or anyone else, are guilty of tolerating error.

Packer defends ECT and also makes the definitive case for evangelical involvement when he argues,

> Contrary to misrepresentations that have got around, it [ECT] does not restrict anyone from presenting the gospel to anyone (the gospel I mean as evangelicals understand it); it only speaks against taking the line that one must change churches in order to be a Christian, while explicitly safeguarding people's right to seek to persuade others that changing churches would be to their advantage.[246]

The naysayers pore over documents like these to discover every possible deviation from what they regard as 'evangelical norms'. So while the *Evangelical Digest* regrets discussions like those of ECT that 'indicate today's regrettable trend away from biblical principles',[247] on the contrary it is *for* biblical principles that evangelical participation in honest theological dialogue is essential.

We have witnessed the trend for evangelicals to become inward looking, and even a strong critic of the Ecumenical Movement, Donald Gillies, says that evangelicals have become 'stricken by the blight of negative criticism and internecine strife'.[248] By looking to themselves, many evangelicals have failed to realize 'that outside of it [evangelicalism] are some of the best saints that God's grace has made', said Rowland Bingham.[249] Mutual recognition among those of like minds, furthermore, is not to be confused with a 'catholic spirit'. Agreeing with those who agree with you is not unity – to the contrary, such a focus can lead to an exclusive mentality.

Iain Murray, one of the recognized leaders of separatism who paradoxically became a minister of a church affiliated with a 'mixed' denomination for a while, wrote in support of evangelical isolationism,

> For Christians to be linked in association with ministers who do not preach the gospel of Christ is to incur moral guilt ... A union which can continue irrespective of whether its member churches belong to a common faith is not fulfilling any scriptural function ... It is error which breaks the unity of churches, and to remain in a denominational alignment which condones error is to support schism.[250]

If Iain Murray's arguments were not logical according to his premise, then he would not have such a considerable following in reformed circles. Nevertheless, this is not the 'catholic spirit' demonstrated by John Wesley or George Whitfield, who endeavoured to remain in a denomination that had many fewer evangelicals than is the case today.

The power that some Christian leaders have can be unhealthy as, for example, the influence of a few articulate spokesmen in some separatist and charismatic circles. Those who would decry the concept of present-day apostles seem to behave like them. By contrast, Paul exercised apostolic authority but was clear about its purpose and limits: 'Not that we lord it over your faith, but we work with you for your joy, because it is by faith you stand firm' (2 Cor. 1:24). Evangelical commentator David Prior says, 'Paul is unambiguously telling the Corinthians "Jesus is Lord, your Lord, and I will do nothing to usurp his pre-eminent place in your lives." That is a searching truth for any person entrusted with pastoral responsibility, because it is all too easy to take the place of Jesus in someone's affections or allegiance.'[251] Yet certain branches of evangelicalism seem to breed dominant leaders who, for example, control what their followers read and discourage contact with wider Christian groups. When leaders express no confidence in the discernment or maturity of their membership, there is a problem.

Certain authority structures in evangelicalism stand in marked contrast to Paul's word to the Galatians, 'It is for freedom that Christ has set us free. Stand firm, then, and do not let yourselves be burdened again by a yoke of slavery' (Gal. 5:1). These barricades have been constructed more recently, for David Bebbington records that the early evangelicals frequently crossed denominational boundaries to meet and consult with each other. This 'catholic spirit' of early evangelicalism and the diversity of expression and emphasis of the New Testament churches express the freedom of which Paul speaks.[252]

As we have seen, interaction among individual evangelicals is increasing, and now is the time for those who are well-grounded in their faith to share it wider still. But, as we are about to discover, that will be a problem for many.

21

Growing Separatist Concerns

Each of us will work out our understanding of the faith in the ways that we live and interact with others, in our worship, and in the ways and places we seek to grow in grace. Those who belong to a church understand and accept their fellowship's statement of faith. Local churches that are true churches exercise a loving guardianship and a holy discipline. I have seen people leave a church after a statement of faith was introduced. That was sad, but there was no alternative. But the members of the church across the road have no such obligation to adhere to my particular statement of faith. What is my relationship to them? And believing, as I do, that the body of Christ is bigger than my fellowship and me, what should my attitude to other Christians be?

I could, of course, choose to extend wider fellowship only to those who express their faith as I do, and whose theology reflects my own. That's simple and safe and saves a great deal of time and trouble. But is that being true to Scripture (e.g., Rev. 2 – 3) and Christ's call? Another historical event of some significance sheds some light on this question for us.

Progress ... or *permixtus*?

A year after Westminster 1966, the Keele Evangelical
Anglican Congress (KEAC) took place. KEAC was called
to give direction, confidence and an agenda to the growing
evangelical constituency in the Church of England.
Different people have assessed the congress according to
their own perspectives. The mainline view is that this was
'the chief landmark in a postwar Evangelical renaissance'.[253] But the separatist view was that KEAC was what
'a former generation [of evangelicals] would never have
countenanced: namely, that the church/denomination is
permixtus in the sense that traditions other than evangelicalism belong in that body alongside our own', said
Graham Harrison.[254] For Harrison and others, KEAC was a
'*permixtus*' – which is an academic way of saying there was
compromise. And so this coming together of churches
from differing traditions in conference further polarized
evangelicals. What was the Council of Jerusalem (Acts 15)
all about?

From such accusations of evangelical compromise
came catchphrases like 'guilt by association' and 'second-
degree separation'.[255] Peter Masters, minister of
Spurgeon's Tabernacle, London, puts the argument as follows:

> Should we separate from Evangelicals who wilfully and
> enthusiastically fellowship and co-operate with false teach-
> ers such as liberals and Catholics? Many Evangelicals who
> themselves maintain biblical separation from those who
> repudiate the true gospel are perplexed about how they
> should regard other Evangelicals who go out of their way to
> co-operate with these false teachers. Should they break fel-
> lowship with them as well? Is what is called 'secondary sep-
> aration' right or wrong?[256]

Masters, perhaps separatism's most cogent and influential spokesman, goes on to give reasons why he believes mainline evangelicals are guilty of 'guilt by association'. He argues that they deal a blow to the exclusive nature of the gospel. They aid the devil by hindering the world from recognizing distinctive biblical Christianity. They lower the guard and expose the faithful to 'the extreme danger of infiltration' and 'they encourage and strengthen false teachers'.[257] A group of like-minded separatist ministers meeting at Hinkley and subsequently at Rugby in the mid-1980s said:

> We declare our intense sorrow that some of our fellow ministers who affirm the same doctrinal truths nevertheless compromise them by failing to speak out against and separate themselves from those who deny these truths and undermine them. Such failure hinders our ability to stand together with these brethren for a clear witness to the truth.

What is the theological answer to opinions like these? Unless there is a cogent answer, the logic of the argument demands a response of acceptance. And, if we accept this, the search for evangelical unity, or any other unity for that matter, is in vain.

All in vain?

It is interesting to note an overlap between some conservative evangelical and Roman Catholic views. Martyn Lloyd-Jones argues that 'Nowhere in [Jesus' prayer in John 17] is there an exhortation or an appeal to *produce* a unity.'[259] Jesus is praying to his Father to 'keep them in a unity that already exists.' Is, then, the whole ecumenical exercise a worthless one?

Similarly, a Roman Catholic explains why that church is not part of the WCC:

> The reason for this abstention is that the Catholic Church is unique in western Christendom in believing that there can be only one Church and that this Church is a single visible organic society alone possessing the fullness of Christ's authority in the world, and that this is the Catholic Church.[260]

For the conservative evangelical there is 'only a unity amongst those who are regenerate or born again'[261] and I would agree with Lloyd-Jones – all evangelicals would. But there is a problem. For Henry St John, the church is the society that possesses 'Christ's authority in the world'.[262] As we have seen, the one Spirit permeates the one body of the church – a spiritual and physical reality – but no-one is able to discern its true membership.

But this position poses a problem. For a separatist in particular, how can there be unity within doctrinal diversity? There is an inconsistency in the separatist argument. Klaas Runia, a separatist theologian, argues, 'The entire New Testament never speaks of unity as such, but it is always a qualified unity. It is always characterized and determined by faithful adherence to the word of the apostles. It is always a *unity of truth*.'[263] Without truth, separatists insist, there is no unity. Unity is in truth, they say, and is a necessary feature of the inherent unity of the church as the body of Christ.

We must presume that no-one perpetrates 'error' for its own sake. Only darkness would *seek* to divide the church. The separatist concern is not diversity in the church, either, for that is inevitable. There are different standards of discipline and forms of government and different hermeneutical methods and doctrines, even among evangelicals. While these differences can actually serve to expand God's king-dom, since a variety of styles draw different people to Christ, people's (sinful) reactions to others with different views have done immense damage to the life and witness of the church.

Separatists lament the frequent use of John 17 in ecumenical circles. Hedegard argues the Jesus is praying for the unity of believers, not churches. Rather optimistically (and perhaps naively) he says, '*then* there was only one Christian church in the world, now a great many churches of differing character … the *unity of churches* is something quite different from the *unity of Christians*'.[264] The distinction that Hedegard seeks to draw is at best tenuous, for believers are the church and the church is a plurality of believers. The New Testament refers to the unity of the church as a fact without qualification. And yet it is for the unity of the church in truth that Christ prays (Jn. 17:17, 21–22). I have 'chapter and verse' to defend my own understanding of truth and I can smell heresy a mile away, but Scripture and experience have taught me that truth is bigger and wider than me and my comprehension of it.

Even when cogently argued by separatists, the unity in truth of which they speak is a pipe dream. If truth is a prerequisite for unity then it is no more attainable for conservative evangelicals than for anyone else, separatists included. The theology that separates the Free Church of Scotland from an Elim Pentecostal church would superficially appear to be as vast – at least pragmatically – as between a main-line evangelical and a convinced Roman Catholic. Neither is theologically liberal, each seeks objective authority, but the gulf separating them is immense. Church unity does not begin by defining truth, though that is essential. It begins with the fact that the church is one. All *praxis* begins there. And on that basis we approach and treat each other differently.

Sometimes it is difficult to differentiate between separatist thought and practice. Separatists profess to have a dread of schism and are sensitive to its charge. Martyn Lloyd-Jones, in his 18 October 1966 sermon, said, 'It is not schism to leave a Church which is apostate – that is one's Christian duty. Schism as defined in First Corinthians is division amongst members which is not sufficiently important to justify division.' In fact, says Lloyd-Jones, 'In the light of that biblical teaching the only people guilty of the sin of schism at the present time are Evangelicals.' Neither does Lloyd-Jones skirt the logic of his argument: 'People who do not believe in the essentials of the faith cannot be guilty of schism; they are not *in* the Church.'[265] But he does not specify what these essentials are, or what the irreducible minimum to be a Christian is. On these points there is a great diversity of opinion, even amongst evangelicals.

Graham Harrison insists that main-line evangelicals are equivocal as to the nature of the gospel. He says, 'If in effect we go on to convey the impression, or worse still explicitly affirm it, that evangelicalism is but one expression of the gospel among several, we have done something more than acknowledge our own humility. We have in fact denied the gospel.'[266]

Main-line evangelicals need to stand for the truths that they believe in the wider church arena. They believe that they have something to say which the church needs to hear, as well as something to receive in return. 'We have a responsibility to share with others', argued David Coffey after the BU voted to stay in membership with CTE.[267] Rather than seeing this as a compromise, evangelicals believe it to be their responsibility.

Harrison concedes the weakness of his position when he says that 'an awareness of our own proneness to wander intellectually, demands that we say as much'. Having admitted such a thing, even reluctantly, leaves separatists no option but to address the matter of unity within a diversity of belief and practice amongst themselves as much as in other Christians. And that is all anyone can ask for – a humility that seeks to give and to listen to people who understand truth differently but with equal integrity.

Diversity without division?

The Scottish theologian John Macquarrie suggests some ways forward that would be difficult for separatists but which the 'confession' of Harrison demands that they undertake. Macquarrie says that 'diversity is just as essential as unity to the well being of the Christian Church'.[268] He draws a distinction between diversity and division when he argues that diversity is difference – different belief, liturgy and spirituality, something that he feels is to be prized and maintained – while division is marked by pride, exclusiveness and bigotry. In that sense, not only separatists but the entire church is liable to schism! 'Diversity is to be maintained, division is to be overcome' Macquarrie says.[269]

Macquarrie makes a fundamental point when he argues that there are different sorts of unity contained between the church's original and ultimate unity. The beginning or origin of church unity, says Macquarrie, is that given unity that is Christ Jesus, which centres in him and comes from him. The end of church unity is what Macquarrie describes as an 'eschatological unity', which is the 'ultimate unity of all mankind in the kingdom of God'.[270] Evangelicals have tended to think that what lies between the beginning and the end has to be a united continuum. They have only been able to conceive of one unity, but this is a denial of reality. Can an evangelical argue that there was no church between the New Testament period and the Reformation? Of course not!

Between Pentecost and the church's ultimate unity in the Godhead is Christ's promise that 'I will build my church' (Mt. 16:18). This pilgrimage for the church is protracted and complex. Christ prayed for the church's unity and Christians must work for its unity – not as an end in itself, 'but that the world might believe' (Jn. 17:21). I am sorry to keep repeating it, but that is what Jesus says.

I would agree with those who argue that ecumenism has become syncretistic, politically suspect, doctrinally indistinct and confused. But these same adjectives could be used to describe many evangelicals. I think there came a point when ecumenists realized something of the problems with ecumenism themselves and did something about it. And that is the responsibility evangelicals now have, too – not just to shake their heads and wring their hands, but to address the disunity which is a denial of what we believe the church to be and a hindrance in its witness to the gospel. What we need is a clear evangelical witness.

IV

The Way Forward

22

A Clear Evangelical Witness

Let's think in a little more depth about evangelical unity before we branch out more widely. As we have seen, the main division between evangelicals does not (as some would imagine) involve the charismatic question. Rather, it is between Christians in the independent or separatist traditions and what I have euphemistically described as 'main-line' evangelicals. Evangelicals can only speak positively into other expressions of the church if they do so with a clear voice, articulating their convictions unequivocally.

This clear witness to evangelical 'truth' is becoming an endangered species, however, as evangelicals seem increasingly unsure of what it means to be an evangelical. Take the recent debate on substitutionary atonement, for example. Apparently what was true of evangelicalism thirty years ago is not necessarily so today. People have changed and convictions have changed. Although these shifts create new problems, the problems should still be addressed. It will not do to throw up our arms in dismay and run away.

Evidence indicates that there is increasing separatist unease towards even the most conservative of main-line evangelicals. The Proclamation Trust runs a training institute for preachers and hosts an annual conference for evangelical ministers based at St Helens, Bishopsgate, London that has been the focus of some displeasure by separatists.[271]

'So Anglicans who never met in fellowship with their non-conformist brethren (except when they were asked to speak) … began yet another conference "to tackle the sad division between Anglican and Free Church Minister,"' said one influential separatist. The tone of pain, rejection and even bitterness is clear. That this legitimate constituency within the church feels so alienated even from other conservative evangelicals is problematical for anyone hoping for constructive unity.

The separatist Alan Gibson expresses some of their legitimate concerns. Regarding statements of faith, he says, if others 'are either to use them as flags of convenience which are not enforced too seriously, or to exploit them by an appeal to hermeneutics which justifies different, yet contrasting interpretations of mental reservations, they can be no basis for constructive relationships'.[272] It is important, therefore, that all evangelicals seriously consider separatist viewpoints. 'The valuable science of hermeneutics is sometimes being abused to justify using the same evangelical language, with different and conflicting meanings,' says the EA.[273] An amalgam of theological viewpoints or doctrinal indifferentism will not be effective in the ecumenical debate.

Separatists suffer now as main-line evangelicals did before them. Whereas non-evangelicals once perceived evangelicals to be irrelevant, main-line evangelicals and others now seem to similarly assess those in the separatist traditions. Modern histories of the church seem hardly to acknowledge the existence of separatists. In the index of *A History of English Christianity*, under 'Free Churches', Hastings lists references to every conceivable Christian group, from Unitarians to Churches of Christ, from the Peculiar People to the Brethren, from Elim to the Black Churches. Yet there is no reference to the FIEC, an organization whose membership includes a significant number of

Free Churches and which is an important part of the evangelical constituency.

Separatism does not fare much better in books from an evangelical standpoint. David Bebbington has but two references in his important history. Derek Tidball says that separatists 'demonstrate a great suspicion about the spiritual credentials of any church but their own' and have 'backed themselves into an evangelical cul-de-sac'. Tidball also says that separatism 'seeks to resist change by insulating itself from the mainstream church' and is 'sectarian in nature', 'idealises the past' and 'fails to have any major transforming influence on society'.[274] If these types of comments sound familiar, it is perhaps because Tidball remembers how others have similarly described evangelicals in the mainstream denominations. Main-line evangelicals need to hear separatists and to appreciate some of the considerable strengths they have to offer.

There are gifted separatist leaders and several strong separatist churches, with representatives from the heart of London into rural areas. Separatists emphasize systematic, expository preaching which develops congregations of theologically articulate people, often within the ambit of the reformed tradition. People like Sir Fred Catherwood, one time vice-president of the European Parliament, and Lord McKay, a previous Lord Chancellor, belong to this tradition. They have virtually no interest in denominationalism but focus on the centrality of Scripture, the person and work of Christ and a 'word-centred' preaching ministry.

The ministries of these churches are *for* truth, and against perceived error. The metaphors of warfare suit the more ardent separatists well, as seen in the subtitle of Ian Murray's biography of Lloyd-Jones, *The Fight of Faith*. They battle not only against the devil and the manifold errors of the wider church, but also against the perceived compromise of main-line evangelicals. Partly because several of their ministers, often Baptists, have seceded from main-line churches over some controversy or another in the past, they are particularly negative towards those whom they believe to know the 'truth' but fail to act upon it by separating themselves from known error. Yet it is only people with strong biblical convictions who can speak to other people with strong biblical convictions with integrity, forthrightness and grace.

Separatists campaign for their position through organizations and publications. A few would reach out to mainline evangelicals. The majority would not support a Billy Graham-type cross-denominational evangelistic initiative because of the possibility of confusion as to the nature of the gospel and compromising their stance by fraternization with other Christians. FIEC ministers, by and large, do not attend local ministers' fraternals or 'fellowship' with neighbouring evangelical churches in the main-line denominations. A few are charismatically inclined. They avoid anything that smacks of ecumenical involvement. Independent evangelicals believe that the truth matters and is to be defended at all costs. Nevertheless, they are prone to certain weaknesses that could in time endanger their very existence.

It is difficult to envisage the source of future separatist growth. Though they understand this for themselves, they address it with a 'spiritual' defensiveness. Geoffrey Thomas, an independent Baptist minister, says of the constituency, 'there is a proper modesty and unassumingness ... Deciding whether they would have many members and much money and read about themselves in the newspaper those churches have decided to promote a growing love for preaching and application of the whole Counsel of God.'[275] Yet in measure these things have also created a people who are self-conscious, inward looking and hesitant to move outside of permitted parameters, which can in turn lead to the 'ghetto mentality' to which Tidball refers in *Who Are the Evangelicals?*

This is a pity, for many outside the separatist community look to separatist leaders with considerable respect and affection. But the estimation is not reciprocated. Many separatists would be suspicious of John Stott, for example, because of his doctrinal questions concerning conditional immortality and ecumenical statements. James Packer has disappointed separatists because of his conversations with Roman Catholics. And separatists criticize some conservative Anglican evangelical leaders not because of their theology, but because they are Anglicans – according to separatist thinking they know the truth but do not follow it and so face particular censure. For separatists, evangelical and ecumenism are a contradiction that cannot be reconciled. Separatists take books like *The Trojan Horse in the Temple*, with its conspiracy theories, seriously. Ecumenism's purpose, this book maintains, is to undermine the gospel. The book's back cover encapsulates what many separatists want to hear and instinctively believe to be true about the Ecumenical Movement:

> Christians have expressed disquiet with what is popularly known as the Ecumenical Movement, which seeks to bring all Christian denominations and organisations into a universal conglomerate … that there is a *hidden agenda* to the global development of such ecumenism, through which there is a concerted effort to undermine the fact that the Christian Gospel offers the only way to spiritual salvation.[276]

Nothing would convince many in this constituency that this was other than completely true or, if once true, is so no longer.

This emphasis is very different from that of E.J. Poole-Connor, one of their early leaders and a founder of the FIEC. Poole-Connor argued that,

> it is to Him [God] a matter of far greater moment that we
> should worship him in spirit and in truth than that we
> should follow any particular method in so doing (Jn.
> 4:21–24) … He pays not the slightest attention to the party
> walls that we so carefully build up. Anglicans or Brethren;
> Denominationalists or Undenominationalists; all who 'hold
> him Head' are alike used and blessed.[277]

How many ministers of FIEC churches would agree with
Poole-Conner today? Instead of fighting 'the world, the
flesh and the devil' separatists appear to be waging war
against the church of which they are a significant part.

In a tolerant age, and under the guise of a misplaced gra-
ciousness, it is right for all evangelicals to point to the danger of diluting or confusing the truths for which they stand.
Structured ecumenical involvement requires more than
language of evangelical tone and spiritual platitudes.
Neither is it a matter of leaders, people and churches getting on well together. Friendship and truth are not the same
thing and should not be confused.

Evangelicals disagree over so many different matters
that it would seem ludicrous for anyone to imagine that
they are the sole custodians of the truth, the only people of
God. This may seem an obvious concession, but it's quite
important. The evangelical cannot but enter into dialogue
amongst themselves and with others. ACUTE mentions
evangelical disagreements over 'the issues of eternal pun-
ishment, sexuality, ecclesiology, the inspiration of scripture,
etc. as all under debate, with some seeing them as primary
and others as secondary'.[278] I, for example, would defend
some of the above vociferously – but not all – so it's best to
talk about them.

Truth is not only to be believed, it is to be shared with the
world and with the church as well. It was a cold orthodoxy
from which the first evangelicals moved away. John

Wesley's 'methodology' was just that until his Aldersgate experience. To be an evangelical is not only to hold a truth but to further a cause. So a Baptist ecumenical report says, 'truly subject to the Word and truly open to the Spirit they become *means* [italics mine] by which the Lord of the church speaks to the churches'.[279] A biblical, confident evangelicalism must live in mutual openness with others to propagate the distinctive message with which they feel entrusted.

There are historical examples for this case I am making. Charles Simeon, 'the doyen of evangelical clergy', and J.C. Ryle, one-time bishop of Liverpool, belonged to the Established Church – which was just as wide-ranging in its theological attitudes as it is today. Each made a stand for his convictions within the church of his day and made a contribution. Some would argue that Simeon was the one who founded the modern Anglican evangelical constituency. Both men maintained their distinctives within a theologically mixed church to the great benefit of the evangelical cause. Max Warren has said, 'An equal threat to any discovery of true unity is to pretend differences do not matter, whereas the spiritual challenge is positively to enjoy them.'[280] It is difficult to enjoy differences because there is fear – of mysteries, of change. And there is also pride, an unwillingness to be found wrong. It gives the impression that the system is not watertight, and allows for the possibility of change and development. Separatists cannot embrace Warren's challenge. 'Our very commitment to the gospel demands that we do not deny with our ecclesiastical alliances what we affirm with our evangelical voices', says Graham Harrison.[281]

One of the appeals of separatism is that it is the 'easier' option, for separatists do not have to engage with the wider scene. It wastes no time on the often barren ecumenical search and asks very few searching questions of itself. It is not nearly as vulnerable as those sections of evangelicalism which believe that their ministry is to the wider church. And yet, vulnerability is one of the costs of the gospel mandate.

Separatists could not be involved in such a movement without apparent compromise – on the biblical teaching on the unity of the church and its implications. Yet there is compromise. Alan Morrison blithely says, 'Although Christian unity is desirable, and also thoroughly biblical.'[282] This statement implies that the unity for which Christ prayed requires a search, but that to take up that biblical warrant is to become tainted.

Alan Gibson admits that the 'church needs to get its act together', that Christ committed himself to 'its structure by saying "I will build my church."' He admits that 'The ecclesiastical supermarket offers a bewildering complexity of options.' But then he reverts to type when he says, 'support [of the Ecumenical Movement] can be seen to owe more to a popular reductionist theology, a theology which finds the perpetuation of traditional differences simply unnecessary'.[283] If this ecumenical reductionist theology is so 'popular' and 'simple', then why has it not been more successful? A reductionist theology would be the death knell of what is argued here. It is only reaching out to others with the whole council of God that will prove sufficient.

Though a liberal evangelical, C.J. Cadoux shows understanding of Baptist norms when he speaks of the need for 'private judgement'. But separatism does not seem to allow this. Cadoux says, 'this autonomy of judgement is just as real in the case of the Catholic and the Fundamentalist, as it is in that of the Liberal Protestant, for each has to decide, and does decide, by an act of private judgement, between the relative claims of different types of teachers.'[284] If it is private judgement that deems separatist teachings to be correct, are those same separatists able to offer that freedom to others who have come to a different conclusion?

It is a fundamental tenet of Baptist belief, according to the Declaration of Principle, 'that each Church has liberty, under the guidance of the Holy Spirit, to interpret and administer His [Christ's] Laws'. Liberty is extended to each Baptist, whether he or she chooses to be a separatist or not. Freedom is allowed to separatists, but is it conceded by them? Freedom 'carries ... a refusal to co-operate with, or even to accommodate' those other than themselves, says Harrison.[285] Obviously, therefore, the corollary must also be true. Evangelicals within mixed denominations need to be more vigilant for the truth, in order to maintain their stance and witness.

Scripture clearly prohibits compromising the truth. No Christian of any persuasion should do that. Yet there is no passage in the New Testament that counsels a person or a church to separate from a brother or sister in Christ. The passage in 2 Thessalonians 3:6ff., which is often touted as the authority for second-degree separationists, is about idleness – not doctrinal plurality. Revelation chapters 2 and 3 speak against serious heresy within the seven churches, but they contain no injunction for anyone to leave them.

Lesslie Newbigin agrees that 'Separation there must be – for the sake of mission', but continues 'that it cannot be the last word. The Gospel is about God's purpose to unite all things in Christ. The cross is the place at which all of every kind and place are to be reconciled, forgiven, united.'[286] And he must be right – but it will not be without pain.

Dividing ... but not conquering

Here I want to anchor some of the theological debates we have been discussing in personal experience and actual situations. I offer these illustrations, which are not without considerable pain, in order to shed light on the realities of which we are speaking.

After experiencing blessing in a ministry in a church in a small community, I left – and the church split into two. Both churches remained in roughly the same geographical area. That each was a gospel church was hardly the point, for that fact only compounded the problem. What did the village think of these Christians who could not live together? Surely the fact that these people could not worship in the same place spoke louder than any evangelistic efforts.

'Doing' evangelism together does not solve the problem of a divided church but emphasizes it. 'Fellowship in evangelism may not result in solving the problem of solution [the different emphasis of the churches] [brackets original] but it certainly will foster an acute consciousness of the scandal of division.'[287] And who said that? The WCC.

In one part of Great Britain there are probably twice as many churches today as there were thirty years ago. Encouraging? Not quite. For while the churches have doubled in number, the people of God have halved. Undoubtedly, Christians would say that 'truth' was one of the reasons they broke away from established churches. But the result is not what they would have hoped or anticipated. Though a few of these fellowships are numerically strong, they have not in any way turned the spiritual tide in that region – in fact, in some ways this multiplicity of churches has compounded the problem.

Sometimes the motivation for forming a new church is a particular worship style, the impact of a 'charismatic' leader, some secondary truth or perhaps a clash of personalities. The fancy name on their sign often covers the pain of division that is the cost of their new endeavour. And while holy huddles abound, community impact is hard to find. We see this phenomenon right across the nation. As the number of 'gospel' churches grows by painful division, the body of Christ bears the scars. The wounded either retreat to build higher theological barricades or limp through the streets proclaiming their new freedom and joy. The people hear the name of Christ on their lips and turn away.

23

Humility with Conviction

The story of the church, sadly, is one of division, heresy and suspicion. None of this can be dismissed in a phrase or solved by a slogan, yet when the church tries to go beyond platitudes to define the problem or to heal the division, somehow matters just seem to get worse. The historical ecumenical approach says that initiative, structure, enterprise and goodwill can create a unified church that will impress a sceptical world and help to build the kingdom of God. As we have seen again and again, however, evangelicals cannot be part of the WCC's 'world-wide synthesis' because of the convictions they hold. What, then, is the way forward? While separatist evangelicals have maintained that structured ecumenism is a vain task, and therefore a worthless one, others have accepted that evangelicals can and should be part of ecumenism's positive aspects.

Another way

I would like to suggest another position, which I hope is a way forward. What I say here is hardly earth-shattering; in fact, it is painfully obvious! But please think it through with me. The evangelical Frank Colquhoun said, 'The variegated wisdom of God calls for a variety of approach.' For some, even to conceive of the 'variegated wisdom of God' poses a problem. But, as Colquhoun continues, 'even in regard to the great doctrines of the gospel the writers do not all think or talk alike'.[288] And so while it *may seem* obvious, I would like to point out that there are sound scriptural and pragmatic grounds for simply acknowledging that different situations demand different responses. The separatists' blanket refusal to have fellowship with other Christians is biblically unjustifiable. But equally dangerous and unbiblical is a *carte blanche* acceptance of everything described as 'ecumenical'.

As we have seen through history, there are situations in which we can and must work with other Christians, and there are other situations where it is more difficult. Our call is but to try – to open our Bibles, pray and remember to treat one another with humility and respect.

Ours is a fallen church, made up of sinful people. Sin affects not only its behaviour but also its belief, its thought-forms, understanding and practice. We must acknowledge, therefore, that neither evangelical exegesis nor its doctrines can ever be the last word on the subject. While as an evangelical I subscribe gladly and wholly to the great evangelical statements of faith, we have discovered that there has to be flexibility concerning both the understanding and application of truth. Truth is wider, higher and deeper than 'evangelical truth'. Evangelicals ought, without compromise of their own fundamental convictions, to be prepared not only for dialogue, but also to give and receive insights. People of conviction can do this best, and in fact I find it is only when conviction is lacking that any meeting of the minds is impossible. Let me explain.

History's positive lessons

Protestants can agree that the Reformation began an important process of reflection and clarification on the nature of the church. Evangelicals would be wrong, however, to imagine that what began at the Reformation also ended there. The Baptists give us an example of this never-ending process.

Baptists complain that the Reformers did not go far enough. In leaving a word like baptism untranslated and therefore unappreciated as to its doctrinal significance, they impaired the understanding and practice of the church (or so we Baptists think – which makes the point nicely!). Baptists were prepared, at the beginning of the seventeenth century, to take the Reformation further. In no age can the understanding of truth be set in concrete, nor can the contribution of one theological school be the whole expression of truth. For different interpretations arise from other, equally valid, readings of Scripture. So it's best to talk about them, I think.

The value of the 'evangelical revival' of the eighteenth century was that the 'warmed heart' and 'catholic spirit' bridged the gap between widely divergent theological norms and practices. The Wesley/Whitefield debate is, of course, still with us – a debate amongst those who stand on the authority of Scripture and come to different conclusions.

So, too, with the founding of the EA in 1846. It is not that the different understandings were either mistaken or secondary, but that as leaders wrestled with them there grew what all church historians have argued was the first manifestation of 'ecumenical' thought and action. Such an evangelical heritage suggests that we should continue this wrestling with divergent views. We cannot overestimate the value of conviction people discussing their differences in a godly way.

So it was with the rise of the Reformed Movement of the 1950s and 1960s. Many Christians came together into a fresh understanding of the sovereignty of God. Then, with the Charismatic Movement, others felt that God was saying something new. All of these emphases and their literature, conferences and dialogue brought people and churches into fresh understandings of truth. Reflecting this 'variegated truth', some churches and leaders were affected by both movements, others by neither.

And so we hold these things in tension: being passionate about upholding the truth and being tolerant of the convictions of others. Lesslie Newbigin writes the following of the union of churches that formed the Church of South India,

> We have turned our minds resolutely towards the task of making union a reality locally, meeting with patience and love many forces that are for ever trying to divide men from each other, creating the necessary diocesan organization, knitting together the many different strands of separate life and labour, and above all keeping before every Christian mind the purpose of our union – "that the world may believe".[289]

Evangelicals need to be part of a similar process now, firstly with each other and then with people who hold other theological insights and have strong convictions. Some will need to form the sort of 'diocesan organization' that Newbigin describes. Others will associate more naturally in loose affinities of like-minded churches. I have to admit that I have never thought the concept of an 'independent' church to be biblical. That conviction has mapped out my career as a minister of the gospel. But, regardless of our different convictions, the patience and love will, and must, still be there.

What is a 'catholic spirit' today? It is the changed life, the 'warmed heart', growth in grace, a godly life, doctrinal conviction, social relevance and evangelistic concern. All of these should mark, but are certainly not only exhibited by, evangelicals.

Evangelicals need to demonstrate this spirit by sharing the lessons of their history and experience. Not, let it be said, in some formal ecumenical conference – history says these achieve very little – but rather with other Christians in the context of study, prayer and joint concern for the spiritual needs of their communities.

The main things are the plain things

In some areas evangelicals are the best able of all Christians to model flexibility. Evangelicalism is not nearly so cluttered with pragmatic difficulties and niceties as the wider church. Take, for instance, the matter of inter-communion that is such a key issue in the ecumenical quest.

Men like William Temple endured terrible heart-searching in areas such as inter-communion. At the coronation in 1953, the Moderator of the General Assembly of the Church of Scotland was not offered communion – something that is hard to believe today. A WCC official said that inter-communion was a subject 'packed so full of emotional dynamite that we are afraid lest poking into it should strike a spark that would blow our whole movement to pieces'.[290]

Leaders including Archbishop Fisher and Professor G.W.H. Lampe of Cambridge expressed the desire that Christians could fellowship and worship and celebrate oneness in Christ together. Most evangelicals welcome all who 'love the Lord' to the 'Lord's Table'. A common recognition of one another in Christ has led many evangelicals to a freedom from denominational labels and the legal restraints of church order and polity. It is by contact that evangelicals can show that the 'spirit' of the matter is more important than the letter.

And yet, the apparent evangelical intransigence on the authority of Scripture seems to be a permanent complication to inter-church convergence. But it need not be a fatal one, for evangelicals are not the only ones to have a 'high' view of Scripture. It would be disingenuous to imply that only evangelicals think biblically. It is important for mature evangelicals to make the most of opportunities to meet with other Christians to share how and why they handle the Bible as they do. I believe in the power of the word of God to be its own witness. How will people hear without a preacher?

The fear and suspicion we have witnessed through the history presented in this book, and that many of us live with still, can only be overcome by building relationships. And these overtures ought to begin amongst evangelicals themselves.

The primary evangelical contribution to a wider ecumenism will be in meeting other Christians, being apologists for their distinctives at a local level. Lenten Bible Studies, for example, provide just such an opportunity. How can a true evangelical ever resist the opportunity to meet others with an open Bible?

There is a great need for committed evangelical apologists who can speak to other constituencies. Neither must this apologetic be merely in the area of doctrine. We witness to our faith in the world and by godliness. It was not an evangelical who said 'Unity must be a unity in truth and holiness', but a previous Archbishop of Canterbury. While evangelicals have emphasized the former ad nauseam, they have been negligent of the implications of the second. Separated Christians cannot be holy if they are complacent in regard to a broken church.

No evangelical would, however, believe that any lasting unity could be established where fundamental differences are avoided by diplomatic evasion or ambiguity. Evangelicals can help to counteract this. Rapprochement requires honesty and personal contact.

Where does unity begin? As we have said, evangelicals must first build confidence amongst themselves. Joint Bible studies, working together on local civic concerns, united prayer meetings and evangelistic initiatives are all areas of godly activity that evangelicals can and do engage in together.

And what should unity be like? Christian unity is a deep fellowship, within the family of God, in a common experience of the gospel of Christ. Although evangelical unity has never attained this ideal, fellowship can be experienced at different levels. 'But if we bow in all humility before the same Lord we ought to be able to present the truth as we believe it, in love and humility, and to be ready to listen to those who differ from us, in a common search for the Truth', says A.T. Houghton, who suffered much criticism for his ecumenical convictions.[291] This is a never-ending process of building contact and trust and working together on mutually acceptable initiatives. Christian unity is not so much a task to be undertaken as a life which must be lived within the church.

Unity: How? And by whom?

The church has become so fragmented, due in large measure to the varied reactions to ecumenism, that what evangelicals really need is an 'ecumenical movement' amongst themselves to build mutual confidence and understanding. But how? And by whom?

The problem with charismatic ecumenicity

Evangelical charismatics within main-line denominations have a unique contribution to make, for they have been able to promote unity both locally and nationally. Peter Hocken has noted that, 'for many grassroots Christians, participation in charismatic prayer meetings was their first experience of fellowship across church boundaries'. And nationally, 'as the charismatic movement spread across the churches, most of its informal structures took an ecumenical form ... In Britain, the Fountain Trust (1964–80) established by Michael Harper to serve the charismatic movement in all churches, served as a model.'[292] Evangelical conviction, however, is more than fellowship with people who testify to a similar spiritual experience.

Contemporary evangelical theologian David Wells describes 'renewal' movements as 'forms of evangelicalism that are not primarily theologies'. Rather than charismatics establishing links on a shared confession they do so 'on the basis of a shared spiritual experience'. In my experience this is, on the whole, true. Many independent evangelicals, furthermore, are deeply suspicious of the Ecumenical *and* Charismatic Movements, and so neither is likely to be accepted as a blueprint for building bridges of trust over the gulfs of Christian antipathy and suspicion.

The role of main-line evangelicals

Because of their doctrinal convictions and wide-ranging contacts with the various strands of evangelicalism, evangelicals within the main-line denominations have a key role in fostering unity. They meet independents and separatists at such conferences as Keswick and through the independent missionary societies, and they meet charismatics at such organizations and events as the EA, Spring Harvest, Soul Survivor and so on. But sadly many of these people are ill prepared and too busy with a multitude of enterprises to make an agenda for unity a priority.

Main-line evangelicals hold many of the theological convictions of the separatists and are less threatened by the 'experience' and worship styles of the charismatics than in the past. After all, they too are people of spiritual experience. This combination of distinctives gives main-line evangelicals a unique opportunity that they must take for the benefit of the whole church.

John Stott has given a lead for a whole generation – not only for Anglicans, but for all main-line evangelicals. Stott has been able to have ecumenical connections while, in the main, keeping the confidence of the evangelical constituency. This is no mean achievement. Other than J.I. Packer, now in Canada, there are few evangelical leaders with the theological profile to follow Stott's example. Both of these men are now elderly, and in any event the unity of the church will not be achieved by a few able, prominent individuals. This is an agenda for which all evangelicals must take some responsibility for themselves.

Sadly, some sections of evangelicalism have majored on the comparatively insignificant, to the detriment of the influence that they could have brought to bear on the whole church. 'Toronto blessings' and a shift towards American-type fundamentalism with 'prosperity' overtones have little intrinsic British appeal. Healing a fractured church is far more pressing. The first modern evangelicals engendered an 'activism' that addressed not peripheries, but the core needs of individuals and communities. In order for evangelicals today to do the same, they will need to free themselves from being locked-in to a system, to cease trying to conform to an ideal and chasing after irrelevancies. They will need to rediscover their place in the whole church and see their authority for this role in Scripture.

Though evangelicals champion a Pauline emphasis, they forget Paul's determination not to be associated with parties and labels. Evangelicals need to be reminded that Paul's faith was not in a 'testimony' or an experience alone, but in a historic event, namely the resurrection, and it was this that drove him forward (1 Cor. 15:3–4). Paul laid claim to no party title in the church. In fact, he constantly derided such things (1 Cor. 3:20–23). For him, truth was centred in the historic work of Christ, applied and experienced personally, expressed in the whole church and then extended to meet the needs of his godless society. Truth was not, and can never be, an end in itself.

Unfortunately, certain strands of evangelicalism seem to have forgotten this biblical picture of the gospel's outworking – to the detriment of their wider church relationships. Evangelicalism is not a movement for itself, or even for 'truth', but is rather an objective testimony to the activity of God in the world and in the church (Mt. 28:19; 2 Cor. 5:19). And the activity of God is demonstrated primarily through the church. The onus is on each one of us, therefore, to work towards the healing of God's church.

24

The Incarnate Church

Living with differences

Let me begin with two stories. On the hill of the Berkshire village where I began my ministry was a delightful Norman church. Every Thursday, the vicar and I met there to say Evensong. One week he was the minister and I was the congregation, and the following week we switched. When the lessons for the day were read we would discuss what the passages were saying. They were some of the loveliest times of my ministry. The vicar was not an evangelical – I don't think he knew what he was. Had I adopted a doctrinaire attitude to ecumenism, I would have completely missed out on this relationship and this giving and receiving with him. But there was more to it than that. Each week before we began our little service he would ring the church bell.

'Why?' I asked. 'No-one ever comes.'

'To tell the village that the ministers are praying,' he replied.

And at 5 p.m. on a Thursday, more villagers than we realized listened out for the bell. People knew that our meeting was right and that somehow it was important for them. And indeed it was, because we prayed for them. Was that ecumenism or gospel opportunity? I didn't really care what others thought – I knew it was right. This for me was a conviction thing, and its fruit was incalculable. It is this sort of contact that I have in mind and for which I am arguing here.

My second story is of a splendid independent church which, in seeking to know the way forward at a church meeting, split its members into groups to hear their ideas and hopes for the future.

'We want to meet other Christians,' was the common reply.

Many Christians share this instinctive longing for wider fellowship – they want to meet others in the family and they feel frustrated when leadership is either careless about, or negative towards, the problem of a divided and hurting family of Christians beyond themselves.

When Christians do come together, they will inevitably disagree over certain points of doctrine or inferences that have been drawn out of a discussion. Some will say these have gone too far and some not far enough. But it is clear that Christians need not to address each other but to talk with each other to build bridges and confront the issues that have divided them. This meeting together is what it means to be the family of God. These 'family reunions' will not occur in the context of ecumenical structures. But what evangelicals were able to do before the EA was formed in 1846 they can do again. Because we recognize the church to be concrete and real, we encourage meaningful conversation between its various parts (1 Cor. 12:24–26).

Talking together

I have used the word 'conversation' rather than dialogue on purpose. Although dialogue is an 'in' word in ecumenical circles, it can cause confusion. There are certain cardinal truths that an evangelical will not be willing to concede in the give-and-take of a dialogue. But all who are involved in a conversation have opportunities to respond, explain and clarify – as well as to listen.

As we have seen, true rapprochement cannot be built if doctrine or issues of substance are avoided. The 'Life and Work' movement posited that doctrine divides – but its neglect has certainly not built unity. This kind of thinking led to the veritable destruction of the Ecumenical Movement. The creeds of the church, the fundamentals of the faith, are the basis of the church's unity. They are the reason and opportunity for evangelical participation.

It is interesting to note that, when we look more closely, very few of the divisions within main-line Christianity have had anything to do with doctrine. Rather, they have often had to do with church government, styles of worship, relationship with the state, and personalities – anything but biblical verities. These are all things we can discuss.

Christians have, of course, always disagreed over elements of doctrine, and in these areas we must maintain humility, for no book or conference is going to resolve these differences now. History, sentiment and prejudice colour all of these points of disagreement. The WCC 'Lima' declaration made a better attempt at tackling these issues than evangelicals have given it credit for, and it is worthy of consideration. But addressing differences has never established unity. To achieve unity requires a change of heart. We must stop majoring on the differences and begin by addressing the fundamentals that a Trinitarian Basis allows.

Unity, by definition, declares one faith (Eph. 4:4). Evangelicals believe along with my friend Wayne Detzler that there is 'an elementary body of Biblical doctrine – the deity of Christ, His substitutionary atonement and his resurrection from the dead', and can seek to witness to no less.[293] Certainly the details and expansion of these things are strongly debated, but that is what true conversation should be about. On this Trinitarian foundation all 'confessing' churches can and must stand. This is the faith for which the first-generation Christians were told to contend (Jude 3). When people do so honestly, vigorously and empathetically, trust will grow.

Humility

In *Evangelical Unity* (keep raiding the second-hand bookshops till you find a copy), E.J. Poole-Connor asked, 'Will any man outside Rome have the hardihood to claim that the religious assembly to which he belongs is alone infallible? The very fact that there are divergences should inculcate humility. Poole-Connor's identity does not prove his argument, but it is significant that he was one of the founders of the FIEC. He continues,

> The utmost that anyone can say is that his creed is a statement of Scripture truth as he sees it and, therefore, binding on his own conscience. To attempt to make it binding on that of his brethren, and to exclude them from communion because their interpretation of the 'one faith' is different from his, is to claim for an exegesis of Scripture the infallibility of Scripture itself.[294]

This is the core of the argument, and Tidball confirms it when he writes in *Who Are the Evangelicals?* of the diversity of evangelicals in the ecumenical context:

> It is too simplistic, then, to identify evangelicalism with an anti-ecumenical stance. There is, in fact, a spectrum of views about ecumenism to be found among evangelicals. One end

of the spectrum draws on the more Protestant elements of the Reformation and the other more Catholic elements. Both can appeal to pages of evangelical history for support, but both must realize that circumstances have changed ... in order that they address the ecumenical question as it now is, rather than as it once was.[295]

Beginning with where we are now, then, what might the church look like if every evangelical took one step forward from where they are in seeking unity. For some that will simply mean meeting with other evangelicals. It has been a matter of particular satisfaction to me to see evangelical independents and those in the established church talking together concerning common concerns.

Rather, the call is proactively to seek, to propagate and explain evangelical convictions – as well as to receive in return some of the riches of other traditions that have been lost to evangelicals.

Suspicion

No-one is being asked to accept the ecumenical package *carte blanche*. As we have seen, evangelical fears in regard to the Ecumenical Movement have not been completely unfounded. I know this from personal experience, and the British ecumenical scene seemed a hard, intolerant place for evangelicals 30 years ago. But things change, and so do we. In the light of history, obsessive concerns and phobias about the ecumenical movement look rather ridiculous. Now there are more significant and dangerous windmills to tilt at. Nevertheless there remains a tension of perception here. Ecumenical fears have sunk deep into the evangelical psyche. Even if some evangelical concerns seem far-fetched to others, we need to acknowledge them and tread gently if ever there is to be a meeting of minds. But the real debate for evangelicals, if and when the ground is cleared of suspicion, misunderstanding and malice, is still a theological one.

'Opportunity by association'

In looking wider than themselves for some basis of spiritual rapprochement, there are undoubted difficulties for evangelicals. Not for a moment do I anticipate that this will be the role of all. But for those Christians who feel able and confident, I would offer encouragement. According to Paul, we search for unity until we reach 'the unity inherent in our faith' (Eph. 4:13, NEB). That search concedes nothing that is essential. Yet there is no reason for anyone *not* to articulate their convictions. Roman Catholics have never conceded what they deem to be essential and no-one would expect evangelicals to do so either.

Evangelicals will be seeking both to explain and convince others of their theological convictions and understandings. This does not argue theological ambiguity, but in fact the reverse. We give the reason for the hope within us.

When someone denies a theological basis, it is not helpful for evangelicals to bemoan the fact at a distance. Making contact creates an opportunity to state objections from the inside. When some joint initiative is taken with which evangelicals cannot agree, or which compromises their distinctives, then they courteously explain why they cannot take part. In this way, understanding and respect can grow. I have called it 'opportunity by association' – and it is the antithesis of 'guilt by association'.

One of the churches of which I was minister was a member of the town's Christians Together group. The church played a part in those activities where it could with integrity and declined to do so when it could not, courteously explaining the reasons why. One such was an evangelistic initiative in which there was little confidence in the message of the missioner. We took the opportunity to explain our hesitancy. The positive contribution this interaction made was far more significant than that of those congregations who refused to be identified with other Christians who didn't agree with them. I believe that Christ was honoured and pleased by the stand we made and the manner in which we conducted ourselves.

But, as you have gathered, my overriding concern is evangelical unity. Among evangelicals, too, it is essential to meet and discuss differences. Recently in England there has been a major and serious theological dispute concerning substitutionary atonement. The EA has sponsored debates concerning the issue to discuss differences. Many attended these sessions because they realized the importance of the issue. But few are prepared for the more protracted, ongoing task of building theological consensus. Strangest of all was the vociferous criticism of the EA amongst some for sponsoring the debates. That Derek Tidball, the chairman of the EA, and general secretary Joel Edwards hold firmly to the traditional – and in my view biblical – position on the atonement does not preclude them from seeking to heal the body of Christ. The matter was of fundamental importance; it had to be addressed, for if other significant leaders had embraced a view that was not biblical it could have attacked the very roots of evangelicalism.

Priorities

We are all busy. But if my theological premise is correct concerning the high priestly prayer of Christ, there is hardly a more pressing agenda than the unity of the church – for it is a springboard to evangelism.

So we press on, Christian people of integrity talking with each other across theological boundaries – jettisoning no conviction, watering down no evangelical tenet of faith, allowing no deflection from conviction. The old Ecumenical Movement is dead – perhaps we need to bury some of the old fears and phobias with it. But, most important of all, we must not let the 'catholic spirit' and 'warmed heart' of early evangelicalism die.

Only misunderstanding and misreporting can ensue if we do not nurture these contacts with other Christians. If we are not proactive at this critical juncture, the sad history of brokenness in the church will repeat itself and continue. We must know what we believe and why, and we must have enough confidence in God and his word to not fear interaction with others. We need to humbly acknowledge that, especially in the area of spirituality, past isolation has meant that there are emphases and insights from other traditions that evangelicalism has lost. We should seek to understand and assimilate some of these. We can identify many areas in which we can share joint concern and responsibility with other Christians – in municipal and social concern, for example, and also in the minefield of legislation that seems to be attacking us from every side. Where we identify with others making a stand for truth, we must stand with them.

The ultimate goal is for evangelicals to build an evangelical ecumenicity amongst themselves, and then with other Christians. Men such as Richard Baxter, with his 'catholic' mind, crossed denominational boundaries in ministerial contact and fraternity. The fruit of his thought and action continues to touch many of us even today. If only we too could touch another generation of Christians, leaving a legacy of unity instead of brokenness.

Lesslie Newbigin wrote the following in his diary about the church of South India: 'It is extraordinarily interesting and rewarding, this process of coming to grips with traditions quite different from one's own, and seeking to test everything by fundamental Scriptural principles.'[296] Unless evangelicals participate in bridge building between themselves and other Christians on scriptural principles, they will have abrogated the name 'evangelical'. Yet if we do not seek to build unity at all, we will have disobeyed Christ's call to us and denied our very name as evangelicals, and we will be robbed of the 'reward' of which Newbigin speaks. Evangelicals believe that the high priestly prayer of Christ was real and for a purpose. He prayed for the healing of the church. We have abrogated our responsibilities for its fulfilment too long. This painful and protracted task is not an end in itself but that the world may believe. It is as important as that.

Endnotes

[1] J. Kent, *William Temple* (Cambridge, 1992), pp. 149–50.

[2] J. Buckeridge, 'The "E" Word', *Christianity* (May 2006).

[3] W.A. Visser't Hooft, *The Word 'Ecumenical': Its History and Use* (London, 1954), p. 735.

[4] Visser't Hooft, *'Ecumenical'*, p. 735.

[5] G.M. Fisher, *John R. Mott Architect of Co-operation and Unity* (New York, 1952), p. vii.

[6] D. MacCulloch, *Thomas Cramner* (London, 1996), p. 3.

[7] J.D. Allan, *The Evangelicals: The Story of a Great Christian Movement* (Exeter, 1989), p. 2.

[8] J.R.W. Stott, *What Is an Evangelical?* (London, 1977), p. 10.

[9] C. Brown (ed.), *The New International Dictionary of New Testament Theology*, I (Exeter, 1975), p. 299.

[10] L. Boettner (ed.), *Baker Dictionary of Theology* (London, 1960), p. 200.

[11] UCCF, *The Doctrinal Basis of the UCCF* (Leicester, n.d.).

[12] Boettner (ed.), *Baker Dictionary*, p. 200.

[13] J. Stott, 'Why It Is Still Important to Be an Evangelical', in J.D. Alan (ed.), *The Evangelicals* (Exeter, 1989), p. 141.

[14] D. Bebbington, *Evangelicalism in Modern Britain* (London, 1989), p. 14.

[15] J. Barr, *Fundamentalism* (London, 1977), pp. 28ff.

[16] A.H. Strong, *Systematic Theology* (London, 1904), p. 888.

[17] D.M. Lloyd-Jones, *Christian Unity: An Exposition of Ephesians* 4:1–16 (Edinburgh, 1980), p. 57.

18 J.-J.von Allmen, *Vocabulaire Biblique* (Paris, 1954), p. 55.

19 H. Richard Niebuhr, 'The Disorder of Man in the Church of God', in WCC, *The Universal Church in God's Design: An Ecumenical Study* (London, 1948), p. 79.

20 D. Holloway, 'The Church and Its Unity', in A. Gibson (ed.), *The Church and Its Unity: When Christians Disagree* (Leicester, 1992), p. 76.

21 G. Aulen in WCC, *The Universal Church*, I, p. 59.

22 K. Barth, *The Faith of the Church* (London, 1958), p. 116.

23 D.M. Lloyd-Jones, *The Basis of Christian Unity: An Exposition of John 17 and Ephesians 4* (London, 1962), p. 12.

24 Barth, *Faith*, p. 116.

25 K. Barth, 'The Living Congregation', in WCC, *The Universal Church*, I, p. 71.

26 J.H. Shakespeare, *The Churches at the Crossroads* (London, 1918), p. 116.

27 W. Temple, *Readings in St John's Gospel* (London, 1942), pp. 328f.

28 Temple, *St John's Gospel*, pp. 328f.

29 A.T. Houghton, 'Unity, Truth and Mission', in J.D. Douglas (ed.), *Evangelicals and Unity* (Nashville, 1964), p. 32.

30 Houghton, 'Unity', p. 32.

31 Lloyd-Jones, *Basis*, p. 14.

32 B.F. Westcott, *The Gospel According to St. John* (London, 1882), p. 246.

33 W. Hendriksen, *The Gospel of John* (Edinburgh, 1959), p. 364.

34 D. Hedegard, *Ecumenism and the Bible* (Amsterdam, 1954), p. 35.

35 Barth, *Faith*, p. 116.

36 A. Thompson, *Beyond Fear, Suspicion and Hostility: Evangelical-Roman Catholic Relationships* (Belfast, n.d.).

37 D. Macleod, 'The Basis of Christian Unity', in *Evangel* III.3 (Autumn 1985), p. 2.

38 Shakespeare, *Churches*, p. 118.

39 'On Holy Scripture and Tradition', from 'The World Conference on Church, Community and State', (Oxford, 1937),

quoted in G.K.A. Bell (ed.), *Documents on Christian Unity, 1920–1924* (London, 1946), p. 254.

[40] M.W. Holmes, *The Apostolic Fathers* (Leicester, 1989), pp. 55; 103; 98; 107.

[41] L. Newbigin, *The Reunion of the Church* (London, 1948), p. 128.

[42] B. Till, *The Churches Search for Unity* (London, 1972), p. 135.

[43] J.R. Geiselmann, A Roman Catholic contributor to Christianity Divided (London, 1962), p. 48, quoted by Till, *Churches*, p. 336.

[44] E.J. Poole-Conner, *Evangelical Unity* (London, 1941), p. 121.

[45] T.W.J. Morrow, *Systematic Theology* (Leicester, 1988), p. 671.

[46] P.T. Forsyth, *The Principle of Authority* (London, 2nd edn, 1952), p. 211.

[47] Morrow, *Systematic Theology*, p. 670.

[48] Forsyth, *Authority*, p. 214.

[49] ACUTE has helped to provide such an arena in the area of single issues (e.g., conditional immortality, etc.), but there is no forum where there is a regular meeting to discuss differences.

[50] D. Guthrie, *New Testament Theology* (Leicester, 1981), p. 744.

[51] Newbigin, *Reunion*, p. 23.

[52] Newbigin, *Reunion*, p. 23.

[53] S. Neill, *The Church and Christian Union* (Oxford, 1964), p. 372.

[54] J.T. MacNeil, *Unitive Protestantism: The Ecumenical Spirit and Its Persistent Expression* (London, 1964), p. 345.

[55] J. Stott, *The Contemporary Christian* (Leicester, 1992), p. 181; Calvin, XIV, pp. 312–14, quoted by J. Cadier in The Man God Mastered (Leicester, 1960), pp. 172–73.

[56] E.A. Payne, 'Toleration and Establishment', in G.F. Nuttall and W.O. Chadwick (eds.), *From Uniformity to Unity: 1662–1962* (London, 1962), p. 272.

[57] J. Milner, 'On Evangelical Religion', in I. Milner (ed.), *The Works of Joseph Milner*, VIII (London, 1810), p. 199.

[58] W.R. Ward and R.P. Heitzenrater (eds.), *The Works of John Wesley, Vol. 19: Journals and Diaries II (1738–1743)* (Nashville, 1990), p. 67 (entry for 11 June, 1739, lines 25 to 26).

[59] Payne, 'Toleration', pp. 270–71.

[60] K. Hylson-Smith, 'Roots of Pan-Evangelicalism: 1735–1835', in Brady and Rowden (eds.), *For Such a Time as This* (London, 1996), p. 144.

[61] J.M. Turner, *Conflict and Reconciliation in Methodism and Ecumenism in England 1740-1982* (London, 1985), quoted in Hylson-Smith, 'Roots', p. 143.

[62] S. Pearce Carey, *William Carey* (London, 1923), p. 253.

[63] William Carey to Dr Ryland, 20 Jan. 1807, in *International Review of Missions* XXXVIII, No. 287 (Apr. 1949), pp. 181ff.

[64] C. Calver, 'The Rise and Fall of the Evangelical Alliance: 1835–1905', in Brady and Rowden (eds.), *For Such a Time*, p. 148.

[65] I. Murray (ed.), *Letters of Charles Haddon Spurgeon* (Edinburgh, 1992).

[66] See R. Coad, *A History of the Brethren Movement* (Exeter, 1976), p. 23.

[67] L.C.B. Seaman, *Victorian England* (London, 1973), p. 10.

[68] O. Chadwick, *The Victorian Church*, I (London, 1966), p. 3.

[69] See Calver, 'Rise and Fall', or R. Rouse and S. Neill, *A History of the Ecumenical Movement*, 1517–1948 (London, 1954).

[70] Rouse and Neill, *A History*, p. 62.

[71] Rouse and Neill, *A History*, p. 62.

[72] The whole story is to be found in *Evangelical Alliance Report* (1847), p. 62.

[73] D. Tidball, *Who Are the Evangelicals? Tracing the Roots of the Modern Movements* (Grand Rapids, 1994), p. 89.

[74] E.A. Payne, *The Baptist Union* (London, 1959), p. 143.

[75] Bebbington, *Evangelicalism*, p. 146.

[76] Tidball, *Who Are the Evangelicals?*, p. 40.

[77] J.F. Findlay Jr, *Dwight L. Moody: American Evangelist 1837–1890* (Chicago, 1969), pp. 253f.

[78] Bebbington, *Evangelicalism*, p. 180.

[79] Rouse and Neill, *A History*, p. 345.

[80] Rouse and Neill, *A History*, p. 357.

[81] Rouse and Neill, *A History*, p. 357.

[82] Editorial, *The Missionary Witness* (7 June 1910), pp. 10–11, cited in SIM International, *Unity and Purity: Keeping the Balance* (Toronto, 1983), p. 11.

[83] R.V. Bingham in *The Missionary Witness* (2 Aug. 1910), p. 127, cited in SIM International, *Unity and Purity*, p. 16.

[84] Bingham in *The Missionary Witness* (2 Aug. 1910), p. 127, cited in SIM International, *Unity and Purity*, p. 16.

[85] R.V. Bingham in *The Evangelical Christian* (Feb. 1911), pp. 37–38, cited in SIM International, *Unity and Purity*, p. 18.

[86] A. Hastings, *A History of English Christianity 1920–1985* (London, 1986), p. 219.

[87] T. Tatlow, *Story of the SCM* (London, 1933), p. 189.

[88] Rouse and Neill, *A History*, pp. 447f.

[89] Bell (ed.), *Documents*, p. 126.

[90] F.A. Ironmonger, *William Temple: Archbishop of Canterbury* (London, 1948), pp. 400f.

[91] Kent, *Temple*, p. 97.

[92] A.C. Headlam, *Lausanne Report*, 1927 (Lausanne, 1927), p. 103.

[93] L. Hodgson (ed.), *The Second World Conference on Faith and Order* (Edinburgh, 1937), pp. 15ff.

[94] Hedegard, *Ecumenism*, pp. 76f.

[95] L. Hodgson (ed.), *Second World Conference*, pp. 250ff.

[96] G.K.A. Bell (ed.), *Documents on Christian Unity, 1920–1930* (London, 2nd edn, 1950), p. 16.

[97] Till, *Churches*, p. 205.

[98] Tidball, *Who Are the Evangelicals?*, p. 188.

[99] Rouse and Neill, *A History*, p. 594.

[100] S. Neill, *Men of Unity* (London, 1960).

[101] R. Jasper, A.C. Headlam, *Life and Letters of a Bishop* (London, 1960), p. 277.

[102] Dr Robert Speer, speaking of Edinburgh 1910 from *Jerusalem Report*, I, p. 343. Quoted in Hedegard, *Ecumenism*, p. 108.

[103] Till, *Churches*, p. 198.

[104] Neill, *Men of Unity*, p. 85.

[105] Neill, *Men of Unity*, p. 114.

[106] *Ironmonger*, William Temple, p. 396.

[107] *Ironmonger*, William Temple, p. 396.

[108] *Ironmonger*, William Temple, pp. 396f.

[109] *Jerusalem Report*, I, p. 118.

[110] *Jerusalem Report*, I, p. 115.

[111] *Jerusalem Report*, I, pp. 353f.

[112] Hedegard, *Ecumenism*, p. 120.

[113] Till, *Churches*, p. 198.

[114] Payne, 'Toleration', p. 272.

[115] Till, *Churches*, p. 202.

[116] J. Huxtable, 'Toward Charity and Understanding: 2', in Nuttall and Chadwick (eds.), *Uniformity*, p. 370.

[117] Rouse and Neill, *A History*, p. 412.

[118] Hastings, *A History*, p. 303.

[119] Hastings, *A History*, p. 533.

[120] A. Gibson, 'The Role of Separation', in Brady and Rowden (eds.), *For Such a Time*, p. 277.

[121] BCC, 'The British Council of Churches, a Process, a Prophecy, a Power' (publicity leaflet, The Church in the World, n.d.).

[122] P.E. Hughes, 'Creeds, Confessions of Faith and Churches', in Douglas (ed.), *Evangelicals and Unity*, pp. 79–80.

[123] N. Karlstrom, 'The Churches and the Chaos of the Age', in Hedegard, *Ecumenism*, p. 11.

[124] WCC, Documents of the World Council of Churches (Geneva, 1956), p. 16.

[125] Till, *Churches*, p. 233.

[126] Cf. WCC, The First Assembly of the World Council of Churches (Geneva, 1948), p. 246; *The Friends' Intelligencer* (24 June 1948), quoted in Christian Beacon 20 (1950).

[127] K. Runia, *Reformation Today* (Edinburgh, 1968), p. 67.

[128] WCC, *The First Assembly*, p. 9.

[129] WCC, *The First Assembly*, p. 5.

[130] WCC, *New Delhi Report*, p. 153.

[131] G.E. Duffield, 'Agreeing in the Truth', in Douglas (ed.), *Evangelicals and Unity*, p. 85.

[132] Till, *Churches*, p. 238.

[133] Till, *Churches*, p. 238.

[134] Bebbington, *Evangelicalism*, pp. 251f.

[135] Bebbington, *Evangelicalism*, p. 252.

[136] H.L. Ellison, *Frontier* (summer 1959), pp. 123f.

[137] WCC, *New Delhi Report*, p. 116.

[138] C.H. Hopkins, *John R. Mott, 1865–1955* (Grand Rapids, 1980), p. 689.

[139] W.A. Visser't Hooft, *No Other Name: The Choice between Syncretism and Christian Universalism* (London, 1963), p. 10.

[140] Till, *Churches*, p. 256.

[141] E.R. Norman, *Church and Society in England 1770–1970* (Oxford, 1976), p. 463.

[142] WCC, *Uppsala Report*, p. 32.

[143] WCC, *Central Committee, Canterbury* (1969), p. 277.

[144] WCC, 'Decisions of the Executive Committee of the WCC Regarding the Special Fund of the Programme to Combat Racism' (WCC press release), p. 3.

[145] WCC, 'Decisions', p. 5.

[146] 'The Gospel According to Marx', *Reader's Digest* (April 1993), pp. 33ff.

[147] Bebbington, *Evangelicalism*, pp. 255ff.

[148] A.J. Van der Bent, *The Utopia of World Community: An Interpretation of the WCC for Outsiders* (London, 1973), p. vii.

[149] Van der Bent, *Utopia*, p. 68.

[150] K. Slack, *The British Churches Today* (London, 1969), p. xi.

[151] Kent, *Temple*, p. 113.

[152] Kent, *Temple*, p. 113.

[153] Tidball, *Who Are the Evangelicals?*, p. 183.

[154] A. McGrath, *A Biography of James I. Packer* (London, 1997), p. 32.

[155] Hastings, *A History*, p. 618.

[156] C. Calver, *Where Truth and Justice Meet* (London, 1987), p. 72.

[157] I. Murray, *Dr Martyn Lloyd-Jones: The Fight of Faith* (Edinburgh, 1990).

[158] McGrath, *Packer*.

[159] D.M. Lloyd-Jones, 'The Opening Rally', in A.M. Derham, *Unity in Diversity* (London, 1967), p. 9.

[160] P. Lewis, 'Renewal, Recovery and Growth: 1996 Onwards', in Brady and Rowdon (eds.), *For Such a Time*, p. 178 (italics his).

[161] Murray, *Lloyd-Jones*, pp. 427–9 (italics his).

[162] Lewis, 'Renewal, Recovery and Growth', p. 179.

[163] Report of the EA, *Commission on Church Unity to the National Assembly of Evangelicals* (London, 1966), p. 3.

[164] Derham, *Unity in Diversity*, p. iv (italics mine).

[165] Murray, *Lloyd-Jones*, p. 525.

[166] E. Davies, '18th October 1966', in BEC, *Foundations*, p. 11.

[167] Davies, '18th October 1966', p. 11.

[168] B. Howlett, '18th October 1966: I was there…', in BEC, *Foundations*, p. 16.

[169] Howlett, '18th October 1966', p. 16.

[170] McGrath, *Packer*, p. 155.

[171] G. Thomas, *Foundations*, p. 31.

[172] F. Catherwood, *At the Cutting Edge* (London, 1995), p. 65.

[173] See McGrath, 'The Break with Martyn Lloyd-Jones, 1970', in *Packer*, pp. 154–61.

[174] A. Morrison, *The Trojan Horse in the Temple: The Hidden Agenda of the Ecumenical Movement* (Derbyshire, 1993), p. 46.

[175] J. Hoad, *The Baptist* (London, 1986), p. 132.

[176] McGrath, *Packer*, p. 81.

[177] Not the 'fundamentalists', as John Huxtable endeavoured to describe them at Nottingham. The charge of fundamentalism had been addressed in J.I. Packer's *Fundamentalism* in 1958. For the difference between evangelical and fundamentalist see *Essentials: A Liberal-Evangelical Dialogue* (London, 1988), pp. 90f., or D.G. Blosch, *The Evangelical Renaissance* (Grand Rapids, 1973), pp. 143f.

[178] Tidball, *Who Are the Evangelicals?*, p. 132.

[179] A. Green, in M. Bochenski (ed.), *When Baptists Disagree* (Didcot, 1993), p. 4.

[180] Bebbington, *Evangelicalism*, p. 267.

[181] A. Gibson, 'Connectionalism', in Gibson (ed.), *The Church and Its Unity*, pp. 119f.

[182] M. de Semlyen, *All Roads Lead to Rome? The Ecumenical Movement* (Gerrards Cross, 1991), p. 24.

[183] J.M. Todd, *Catholicism and the Ecumenical Movement* (London, 1956), p. 23.

[184] Todd, *Catholicism*, pp. xii–xiii.

[185] Hastings, *A History*, p. 470.

[186] Payne, *Baptist Union*, pp. 200, 219.

[187] Hoad, *The Baptist*, p. 135.

[188] Hastings, *A History*, p. 541.

[189] N. Goodall, *Unity Begins at Home: A Report of the First British Conference on Faith and Order* (Nottingham, 1964), p. 45.

[190] Hastings, *A History*, p. 548.

[191] Hastings, *A History*, p. 548.

[192] Till, *Churches*, p. 372.

[193] Till, *Churches*, p. 372.

[194] L. Newbigin, *Unfinished Agenda: An Autobiography* (Grand Rapids, 1985), p. 250, cited in Hastings, *A History*, p. 626.

[195] BEC, *Holding Hands in the Dark* (St Albans, 1989), p. 2.

[196] Hastings, *A History*, p. 626.

[197] Hastings, *A History*, p. 627.

[198] D. McBain, *Fire over the Waters* (London, 1997), p. ix.

[199] In a review of *The Faith of the Vatican* by Herbert Carson, an independent Baptist who seceded from the Anglican ministry largely because of ecumenical issues (*New Christian Herald* [29 June 1996]).

[200] The reasons for this are too numerous to discuss here. Figures published in December 2006 state that Pentecostal/Afro-Caribbean churches now outnumber Methodists in the UK.

[201] W.A. Visser't Hooft, *Has the Ecumenical Movement a Future?* (Belfast, 1974), pp. 28f.

[202] Visser't Hooft, *Future?*, p. 29.

[203] NSBP became 'Churches Together' or 'Christians Together' following the conference referred to as Swanwick (so-called after the centre where it was held).

[204] H.J. Margull, 'The Ecumenical Advance,' in H.E. Fey (ed.), *A History of the Ecumenical Movement 1948–1968* (London, 1970), p. 355.

[205] BCC, *Not Strangers but Pilgrims*, p. 1.

[206] Tidball, *Who Are the Evangelicals?*, p. 11.

[207] H. Kung, *The Changing Church: Reflections on the Progress of the Second Vatican Council* (London, 1965), p. 39.

[208] A landline used in the 1950s to bring the Keswick meetings to various centres across the country.

[209] Till, *Churches*, p. 228.

[210] *Catholic Herald* (7 Sept. 1978).

[211] Hastings, *A History*, p. 668.

[212] *The Sunday Times* (16 Jan. 1994).

[213] de Semlyen, *All Roads Lead to Rome?*, p. 24.

[214] Bebbington, *Evangelicalism*, p. 267.

[215] D. Edwards, *The British Churches Turn to the Future* (London, 1973), p. 46.

[216] A. Johnston, *The Battle for World Evangelism* (London, 1978), pp. 299–300.

[217] Johnston, *Battle*, p. 301.

[218] Pan African Christian Leadership Conference, Nairobi 1976, in Hastings, *A History*, pp. 616f.

[219] Hastings, *A History*, p. 617.

[220] J. King, *Church of England Newspaper* (11 Feb. 1977), p. 6.

[221] D. Watson, *Church of England Newspaper* (April 1977), p. 6.

[222] WCC, *The Universal Church*.

[223] J. Charley, 'Church Order', in Derham, *Unity in Diversity*, p. 17.

[224] P. Master and J.C. Whitcomb, *Separation and Obedience* (London, 1983), pp. 9–11.

[225] W. Hendriksen, *The Gospel of John* (Edinburgh, 1959), pp. 362f.

[226] G.K.A. Bell, *Christian Unity: The Anglican Position* (London, 1948), pp. 189–90.

[227] L. Newbigin, *What Is a Local Church?* (Geneva, 1977), p. 21.

[228] F. Colquhoun, *The Fellowship of the Gospel* (London, n.d.), p. 52.

[229] D. Gillett, *Trust and Obey* (London, 1993), p. 38.

[230] A. Morrison, *The Serpent and the Cross: Religious Corruption in an Evil Age* (Birmingham, 1994), p. 546.

[231] Morrison, *Serpent*, p. 546.

[232] U. King, *Towards a New Mysticism: Teilhard de Chardin and Eastern Religions* (London, 1980), p. 226.

[233] D.J. Bosch, *Transforming Mission* (Maryknoll, NY, 1994), p. 383. A chapter called 'Elements of an Emerging Ecumenical Missionary Paradigm' is of particular relevance.

[234] Visser't Hooft, *No Other Name*, p. 10.

[235] K. Slack, *Nairobi Narrative* (London, 1976), p. 78.

[236] 'The Evangelicals of ECONI' (discussion paper; ECONI, 17 April 1997).

[237] D. Prior, *The Suffering and the Glory* (London, 1985), pp. 47.

[238] Till, *Churches*, p. 521.

[239] L. Newbigin, *A South India Diary* (London, 1960), p. 5.

[240] Tidball, *Who Are the Evangelicals?*, p. 31.

[241] J. Lawrence, *The Hard Facts of Unity* (London, 1961), p. 67.

[242] BEC, 'Executive Council' (St Albans, 1986), p. 5.

[243] ACUTE, *What Is an Evangelical?* (London, 1996), p. 3.

[244] Quoted from the anti-ecumenical BEC *Ecumenical Digest* (summer 1996), p. 3, citing *Cross Way*, the magazine of the church society (spring 1996).

[245] *Evangelicals Now* 9.12 (Dec. 1994), p. 7.

[246] *Evangelicals Now* 9.12 (Dec. 1994), p. 7.

[247] *Evangelical Digest* (summer 1995), p. 1.

[248] D. Gillies, *Unity in the Dark* (Edinburgh, 1964), p. 7.

[249] R.V. Bingham in *The Evangelical Christian* (Jan. 1913), pp. 4–5, cited in SIM International, Unity and Purity, p. 10.

[250] I. Murray, *The Forgotten Spurgeon* (Edinburgh, 2nd edn, 1973), pp. 158–59.

[251] Prior, *Suffering*, pp. 46–47.

[252] Bebbington, *Evangelicalism*, pp. 31f.

[253] Bebbington, *Evangelicalism*, p. 249.

[254] G. Harrison, 'Evangelical Separation', in Gibson (ed.), *The Church and Its Unity*, p. 144.

[255] 'Second-degree separation': although someone might be a true evangelical, the faithful must not hold his hand because they do not know whose hand this person is holding. It revolves around 'guilt by association'.

[256] P. Masters and J. Whitcomb, *Separation and Obedience* (London, 1983), p. 6.

[257] Masters and Whitcomb, *Separation*, pp. 7f.

[258] The Hinkley Statement, Clause 4 (unpublished).

[259] Lloyd-Jones, *Basis*, pp. 11f.

[260] H. St John, *The Church and Christian Unity: A Study of the Ecumenical Movement* (London, 1964), p. 40.

[261] Lloyd-Jones, *Basis*, p. 14.

[262] St John, *Church*, p. 41.

[263] Runia, *Reformation Today*, p. 67.

[264] Hedegard, *Ecumenism*, pp. 35f.

[265] D.M. Lloyd-Jones, preaching at the opening of the 1966 EA National Assembly. Published in précis as ch. 1, 'The Opening Rally', EA, *Unity in Diversity*, p. 11.

[266] Harrison, 'Evangelical Separation', in Gibson (ed.), *The Church and Its Unity*, p. 157.

[267] D. Coffey, *Baptist Times* (18 May 1995).

[268] J. Macquarrie, *Christian Unity and Diversity* (London, 1975), pp. 28f.

[269] Macquarrie, *Christian Unity*, preface.

[270] Macquarrie, *Christian Unity*, pp. 2–3.

[271] G. Thomas, 'Then and Now: 1966–1996' in BEC, *Foundations*, citing C. Green and D. Jackman (eds.), *When God's Voice is Heard* (Leicester, 1995), p. 18.

[272] Gibson (ed.), *Church and Its Unity*.

[273] ACUTE, *Evangelical?*, p. 3.

[274] Tidball, in *Who Are the Evangelicals?*

[275] Thomas, 'Then and Now', p. 31.

[276] Morrison, *Trojan Horse*.

[277] Poole-Connor, *Evangelical Unity*, p. 35.

[278] ACUTE, *Evangelical?*, p. 2.

279 BU, *Visible Unity in Life and Mission: Baptist Response to the Ten Propositions of the Church Unity* Commission (Didcot, 1977), p. 201.

280 M. Warren, *Crowded Canvas* (London, 1974), pp. 213f., in Gillett, *Trust and Obey*, p. 3.

281 Harrison, 'Evangelical Separation', in Gibson (ed.), *The Church and Its Unity*, p. 165.

282 Morrison, *Trojan Horse* (back cover).

283 Gibson (ed.), *The Church and Its Unity*, p. 36.

284 C.J. Cadoux, *The Case for Evangelical Modernism* (London, 1938), p. 27.

285 Harrison, 'Evangelical Separation', in Gibson (ed.), *The Church and Its Unity*, p. 165.

286 L. Newbigin, 'When Is a Local Church Truly United?' (paper presented at a WCC consultation on the meaning of the term 'local church'), in WCC, *In Each Place: Towards a Fellowship of Churches Truly United?* (Geneva, 1977), pp. 18f.

287 Poole-Connor, *Evangelical Unity*, p. 77.

288 F. Colquhoun, *The Fellowship*, p. 51.

289 Newbigin, *South India Diary*, p. 26.

290 Douglas (ed.), *Evangelicals and Unity*, p. 10.

291 Houghton, 'Unity', p. 45.

292 P. Hocken, 'Charismatic Movement', in N. Lossky, J.M. Bonino, et al. (eds.), *Dictionary of the Ecumenical Movement* (London, 1991), p. 146.

293 W. Detzler, *Living Words in Ephesians* (Welwyn, 1981), p. 86.

294 Poole-Connor, *Evangelical Unity*, p. 77.

295 Tidball, *Who Are the Evangelicals?*, p. 175.

296 Newbigin, *South India Diary*, p. 50.